FINANCIAL
COUNSELLING

FINANCIAL COUNSELLING

A practical guide to everyday problems

KERRY A. FALLON HORGAN

Allen & Unwin
Sydney London Boston

Dedicated to my husband, Brendan Horgan, without whose practical and moral support this book would not have been possible.

First published in 1987

Allen & Unwin Australia Pty Ltd
8 Napier Street, North Sydney, NSW 2060 Australia

Allen & Unwin New Zealand Limited
60 Cambridge Terrace, Wellington, New Zealand

George Allen & Unwin (Publishers) Ltd
18 Park Lane, Hemel Hempstead, Herts HP2 4TE England

Allen & Unwin Inc.
8 Winchester Place, Winchester, Mass 01890 USA

National Library of Australia
Cataloguing-in-Publication

Fallon Horgan, Kerry A.
    Financial counselling.

    Includes index.
    ISBN 0 04 332131 3.

    1. Finance, Personal—Australia.   2. Budgets, Personal
    —Australia.   3. Debt.   4. Consumer education—
    Australia.   I. Title.

332.024

Set in 11/13pt Century Schoolbook by Asco Trade Typesetting Limited in Hong Kong
Produced in Malaysia by SRM Production Services Sdn Bhd

Contents

Acknowledgments

The knowledge contained in this book is a culmination of eight years' experience in the field of financial counselling and seven years of education in the areas of psychology, welfare and law. It consists of practical ideas and information learnt from experience in the field, as well as from colleagues, clients, teachers and students, all of whom are too numerous to name individually. I am most grateful for the permissions to reproduce documents, and/ or for the helpful assistance given by the NSW Department of Consumer Affairs, the State and Federal Attorney-Generals' Departments, the Family Court of Australia and the Trade Practices Commission.

There are several people who have been of particular importance in the development of this book. The love and guidance of the late Margaret Hughes Connors made a special impact on my life and my way of thinking. The valuable comments given by my colleagues Betty Weule and Narelle Bell greatly enhanced the finished work. Over the years many other colleagues have shared their knowledge and expertise, and I wish to thank Iris Collins, Faye Gornalle, Claire Hogan, Gail Terrassin, David Howard, Gillian Moon, Thelma Waters and Cheryl Dolan. A major contribution to this book was made by Jennifer Gillis, who not only added useful insights and gave much positive support, but generously gave of her time to type the manuscript. My grateful thanks also go to Mary Fallon, who provided her proof-reading skills.

The forms that appear on pages 79, 83, 84, 87, 88, 91, 94, 95, 96, 97, 98, 99, 100, 101, 102 and 103 are subject to Crown Copyright and reproduction is made with the kind permission of the State and Federal Attorney-Generals' Departments. This material may not be published by any electronic or computerised information retrieval system.

Introduction

This book is a practical guide to financial counselling, with an emphasis on consumer education. It gives an overview of the skills and knowledge required by the counsellor so as to assist people who are experiencing financial problems and to help them avoid such problems occurring.

It is what I call a 'whole person' approach to financial counselling. This approach recognises the need to consider the social, emotional, physical, legal and financial aspects of the individual or family situation. It will therefore be of benefit to anyone working with people who are having financial difficulties, and of particular interest to consumer educators and students and practitioners of social welfare.

An ideal financial counsellor would have expertise in counselling skills, the law, accountancy, education and consumer issues. Just as it would be unusual to find this combination in one person, it is impossible to thoroughly explore the avenues open to those with financial problems in this small guide. Therefore this book is a reference or starting point for further exploration. It aims to demystify the field of financial counselling and to help readers ask more questions rather than to provide all the answers.

Legal underpinnings

Various legal areas in relation to financial counselling are considered. These include consumer protection laws, credit legislation, debt recovery procedures and workers' compensation. It is outside the scope of this book to adequately cover the knowledge required in these areas in order to give legal advice to a client.

The purpose is to highlight aspects of the law which are involved in financial counselling and to help the reader to recognise when professional legal assistance is required and as a result be able to make appropriate referrals.

The sources of law in Australia include the decisions of the courts and the legislation made by the parliaments. In general, Commonwealth legislation overrides that of the states and territories, and all legislation takes precedence over case law. Nevertheless an important function of the courts is the interpretation of the legislation and the application of statutory provisions. This book will consider relevant acts of parliament and how they can be used to assist people in financial difficulties, for example, through their application in the courts.

Although Commonwealth legislation is applicable throughout Australia, there are variations in the statutes and delegated legislation of the various states and territories. Nevertheless similar laws will generally be found in the different states and the State laws of New South Wales will be used as the example in this book.

There are several legal reference books which will supplement the information given here and will be of particular benefit to counsellors who are assisting people in financial difficulties. These include the Redfern Legal Centre *The Law Handbook* Sydney: Redfern Legal Centre, 1986; N. Seddon (ed.) *ACT Supplement to the Legal Resources Book (NSW)* (2nd edn) Canberra: the Law Faculty of the Australian National University, 1982; R. Graycar (ed.) *Legal Resources Book (SA)* Sydney: Allen & Unwin, 1981; J.R. Gardiner et al (eds) *Legal Resources Book (Vic)* (2nd edn) Melbourne: Fitzroy Legal Service, 1978; Caxton St Legal Service *Legal Resources Book (Qld)* Brisbane: Caxton St Legal Services Incorp., 1983.

The recent credit laws

In early 1985, Victoria, Western Australia, New South Wales and the Australian Capital Territory implemented new credit legislation. These laws are generally uniform but extremely complex. A detailed examination of the acts and regulations must be undertaken before advice on credit is offered to a client.

The complexity of these laws and the many exceptions to various provisions make it impossible to accurately discuss the acts in simplified terms. I have therefore given a general overview of the laws in three sections, with the NSW Credit Act providing the example.

The protection given to consumers by these laws is broadly covered in Chapter 2, 'Consumerism'. The types of credit contracts regulated by the acts are discussed in Chapter 4, 'Loans and the way they work'. And the assistance given to debtors who are unable to maintain credit commitments is considered in Chapter 7, 'Debt and legal action'.

The new credit laws are to be found in the Credit Acts and various cognate acts as follows:

Victoria

Credit Act, 1984
Credit (Administration) Act, 1984

Western Australia

Credit Act, 1984
Credit (Administration) Act, 1984
Commercial Tribunal Act, 1984
Acts Amendment and Repeal (Credit Act), 1984

New South Wales

Credit Act, 1984
Credit (Administration) Act, 1984
Commercial Tribunal Act, 1984
Credit (Home Finance Contracts) Act, 1984
Credit (Finance Brokers) Act, 1984
Miscellaneous Acts (Credit) Repeal and Amendment Act, 1984

Australian Capital Territory

Credit Ordinance, No. 5 of 1985

References on the new credit laws include:

Bingham, P. *Credit Handbook Your Rights Under the New Credit Laws in Victoria & New South Wales* Brunswick: Globe Press Pty Ltd, 1985.

Levine, J. *New South Wales Consumer Credit Legislation with annotations* Sydney: CCH Australia Limited, 1985.

Levine, J. *Victoria Consumer Credit Legislation with annotations* Sydney: CCH Australia Limited, 1984.

1

Why financial counselling?

In a large percentage of cases if a person seeks assistance from a counsellor or social welfare service, at least part of their problem will be financial. It is therefore essential that students of social welfare and professionals in the field have the ability to recognise the financial aspects of a person's problem and be able to deal with them, or at the very least make an appropriate referral to a financial counselling service.

Any one of us at some time in our lives can experience a financial problem. People of all ages, cultures and income levels, from the well educated to the illiterate, can suffer financial difficulties because of short-term or long-term problems.

The underlying causes of financial difficulties are many and varied. The most frequently encountered are unemployment, illness, marital breakdown, low income, death of a spouse, addictions, business failure, inflation, lack of money management skills, unawareness of consumer rights, psychological problems and materialistic pressures.

The life-crisis situations such as illness and death of a spouse are obvious reasons for financial problems; less evident are the pressures of materialism and lack of money-planning skills. The last two cases can lead to overcommitment through the overuse of credit facilities, such as bankcards, department store accounts and personal loans. Consumers are often taken in by television and telephone advertising and door-to-door sales. Add to this unwise purchasing, compensation spending, lack of knowledge about one's rights and an inability to handle finances, and the reasons for the person's money problems become clearer.

Over many years of counselling and teaching, few people I have encountered, regardless of the level of education, have known how to budget their money. My clients have included people whose only source of income is a pension or benefit, and people working in skilled, unskilled and professional capacities. It is not uncommon to see people who are more than $1000 a month overcommitted, suffering the consequent social and emotional effects.

A common situation is the young couple who marry and decide to buy a house. With unrealistic expectations, immaturity in handling finances and unawareness of consumer rights, they wish to start with all that their parents owned after a lifetime of work. The couple have two incomes but have not saved enough for the deposit and legal costs, which are borrowed at high interest rates. Once in the house they find access to credit easy and with the pressures of advertising and skilled sales techniques they borrow from department stores and use credit cards to purchase furnishings, linen and the microwave. Then of course the new car is needed to keep up appearances in the neighbourhood.

By this stage both incomes are stretched to the limit. Nevertheless they decide it is time to start a family. One income ceases and their whole world comes crashing in on them. The financial pressures possibly result in the breakdown of the marriage, legal action being taken by creditors to repossess the house and household goods, repayment defaults noted on their credit file, garnishee of wages, loss of job and subsequent health problems.

The results of such pressures can be severe and affect not only the individual and family but also the community at large. The emotional and social stress associated with financial problems can lead to family breakdown, feelings of powerlessness and fear, loss of self-esteem, health problems, loss of productivity and possibly loss of job. Also social alienation, psychological problems and in some cases even suicides have been linked with financial problems. The need for financial counselling in our society is apparent.

The practical approach of dealing with the underlying cause of the problem means that financial counselling is effective in helping people gain control of their situation and in learning new skills to prevent future financial problems.

Aims of financial counselling

There are four main aims of financial counselling. These are prevention, skill development, obtaining control of finances and effecting change.

Prevention can be achieved by educating individuals and groups of people about their rights as consumers and about legal issues relating to their debts. The rights of consumers and debtors are discussed throughout this book, starting in Chapter 2, 'Consumerism'.

The development of life skills such as money planning, wise shopping and nutrition means that people can make the best use of limited resources and fulfil more needs and wants. See Chapter 3, 'The money plan'.

Gaining or regaining control over finances is possible by dealing with the underlying cause of a person's financial problem. This is explored in Chapter 5, 'Techniques of financial counselling'.

Financial counselling also seeks to effect change not only on an individual level but also on a social level, for example, by lobbying for changes in consumer legislation. See page 4, 'Financial counsellors' associations'.

Referral to a financial counsellor

Financial counselling agencies differ in the types of services offered to their clients, and in New South Wales the lack of funding means that there are insufficient services and long appointment lists. It is therefore necessary in the first instance to contact the agency to ensure they offer the service required. Financial counselling cannot take place over the telephone as documentation must be read, and an average interview takes approximately two hours. Most agencies require that clients make their own appointments.

Before referring someone for financial counselling, it is important to explain the type of service offered and in particular that loans of money and cash grants are not provided by most services.

Before the interview, clients will need to spend some time writing down a list of their living expenses and fixed commitments. They will need to bring this information to the interview along with any loan contracts, outstanding bills, copies of accounts, income verifications, court documents or letters relating to their financial situation.

Finances are a personal matter and people are often reluctant to disclose their total financial position. It is therefore important to explain why this information is needed. Unless the financial counsellor is given an accurate picture, appropriate alternatives cannot be explored and the person's financial difficulties can even be exacerbated. This can be the case, for example, if the person has more debts than indicated and a repayment scheme is arranged with the creditors which the person cannot maintain. This can result in further financial difficulties if creditors then take legal action. Understandably, creditors are less willing to cooperate a second time if the first arrangement did not succeed because the true facts were not disclosed.

Financial counsellors' associations

Various states throughout Australia have professional bodies whose members have associate or full-membership status. There is also a national association, consisting of individual financial counsellors throughout Australia. Financial counsellors can belong to both a state and the national body.

The Financial Counsellors' Association of NSW and the ACT aims to:

- evaluate the financial problems of members of the community and take up social issues. This is achieved through research, lobbying, support of organisations with similar objectives and liaison with government departments, consumer organisations and other parties in respect of people in financial difficulties.

- provide members with continuing training and current information. Financial counsellors who are members of the Association have a variety of qualifications and experience. They include solicitors, social workers, welfare workers, accountants, educators, community workers, family-support workers and volunteers from various financial counselling agencies. This wealth of knowledge and experience is shared at meetings, through newsletters and on less formal levels. Experts in various fields are also brought in to speak on topics of interest to members. As there are constant changes in matters relating to financial counselling, for example, in consumer legislation, the Association plays a vital role in maintaining the knowledge and standards required of its members.

- establish the required standards in the areas of training and experience before financial counsellors attain full-membership status. At present this status is reached when a person has completed an approved course, has worked as a financial counsellor for at least 12 months and has gained any other qualifications that may be prescribed by the Management Committee. The Association has also developed a curriculum for a short course in financial counselling to be offered in various colleges of technical and further education.

- uphold the ethics of the profession. The Association has developed a code of ethics which is important not only to the practitioner but also to those individuals and organisations interacting with financial counsellors for an understanding of the conduct and standards required by the professional body. The general principles include the provision of confidential and professional counselling, rehabilitation of those in financial distress and the fostering of consumer education in the community in the areas of money management and use of credit. There are also standards of conduct in relation to the individual counsellor, to clients, organisations, colleagues, welfare services and credit providers.

Further information about the Financial Counsellors' Association of NSW and the ACT can be obtained by writing to PO Box A526, Sydney South, 2000.

2

Consumerism

The ways in which people use their financial resources are mainly determined by physical, social, emotional and psychological factors. Some of these influences are apparent, others are intrinsic or subconscious. In financial counselling it is often the realisation of why money is being used in particular ways which will be the key in realistically establishing priorities to make the best use of the resources available.

Once the basic physical needs of food, clothing and shelter are satisfied, money can then be spent on fulfilling the other needs and wants of people. It is here that individual factors must be taken into account. A basic necessity to one person may be a luxury to another, even if they have similar financial resources. The reasons for this are complex and include a combination of factors such as a person's values, standards, goals and life circumstances.

Values include the need for love, security, friendship, marriage, education and health. These values are intangible but are highly motivating factors in determining how people will spend their money. They are initially learnt from parents and are later influenced by peers, schools and important developmental factors, such as religion. Value systems tend to become firmly established in adulthood. Some or all of the values learnt while growing up may never be questioned and are maintained throughout life; others may be evaluated by the person and subsequently accepted, rejected or adapted.

No matter what the value system of an individual, it is usually deeply entrenched and unlikely to be changed. This can lead to dysfunctional behaviour and have adverse effects on a person or their family: for example, a parent who will not touch savings set aside for their children's university education, even though the teenage children do not want to attend university, and as a consequence necessary possessions are repossessed; or the parent who will not accept any board from adult working children even though it may mean bankruptcy. The appreciation of a person's value system can be the first step in understanding why financial resources are being used in a particular way.

Standards are extrinsic motivating forces and are influenced by the media, advertising and society generally. Standards include factors such as hygiene, nutrition, what we wear, location and type of housing, model of car and purchase of luxury items. The sophistication of advertising and high-pressure sales techniques as well as peer pressure greatly determine people's spending patterns. Thus a person may believe that to be accepted means dressing in a certain way, owning a certain car or brick-veneering the house like everyone else in the street. Such standards can lead to overcommitment and subsequent financial disaster. The financial counsellor can assist by helping the person to become aware of these pressures in order to be able to reassess priorities and attain realistic standards.

Goals are influenced by values, standards and life circumstances. They are the conscious choices we make to achieve certain objectives. Financial resources are channelled in a specific direction to reach these goals. For example, a young couple may marry and have the goal of buying a house. This may mean a drastic change in lifestyle and spending patterns in order to achieve this goal. If they have a family, spending patterns may again need to be re-evaluated. When the children start school and then high school, the family's expenditure tends to be at its peak and goals may have to change to include the basic necessities of clothing or an affordable holiday. When the children leave home the goals can be reassessed and may then include the purchase of a luxury item or saving for retirement.

To establish realistic goals it is necessary to explore values and standards and appreciate the stages of life in order to meet current and future needs. It is also imperative that counsellors understand their own values and standards and do not impose these on a client.

There are many other factors which can affect the ways in which people spend their money and the above are just some of the main influences. Other factors, such as emotional and psychological problems, drug addictions and gambling, require specialist treatment and must be dealt with before financial counselling can assist.

Consumer rights

In our society, the consumption of goods and services is seen as a vital part of everyday life and the basis of our economy. Problems with such a system arise when purchases are defective, when consumers are placed in an unequal bargaining position, when they do not know their rights and when they are persuaded to purchase goods they do not really need or even want as a result of high-pressure or deceptive advertising and sales techniques. It is generally the less well educated and the poor who are the most vulnerable consumers and the most likely to suffer adversely in the marketplace.

In an attempt to protect consumer rights in Australia, the Commonwealth and State parliaments have enacted laws which are in addition to the rights found in our common law. These laws include the Trade Practices Act, the Credit Acts, the Sale of Goods Acts, door-to-door sales legislation, the Contracts Review Act and the general law of contract. Even though consumers are given certain rights under these laws, pursuing these rights can be time consuming, expensive and complex, requiring expert legal advice. It is intended here to briefly consider the purpose of the legislation and how it may help consumers, and not to give an exhaustive study of consumer rights and remedies provided by these laws. A helpful supplement to the topics highlighted in this chapter can be found in J. Goldring *Consumers or Victims* Sydney: Allen & Unwin, 1982.

The Trade Practices Act 1974

This is a statute enacted by the Commonwealth Parliament and as such is applicable throughout Australia. Broadly speaking, the consumer protection provisions of the Trade Practices Act relate to the supply of goods as well as to the supply of services provided by corporations. Usually a corporation can be identified if it uses the words or abbreviations 'Limited', 'Ltd', 'Proprietary Limited' or 'Pty Ltd' after the name of the company.

In general a company contravenes this Act if it deceives people about the type, quality, purpose or price of its goods or services. Such misleading claims could be made by the company's sales staff, through its advertising or even by the labelling of its products. Certain other unfair practices are also prohibited by the Act. These include pyramid, inertia and referral selling; bait advertising; misleading predictions about future matters; the sending of unsolicited credit cards; accepting payment for goods or services without intending to provide them; supplying goods that do not comply with product or safety standards; the use of undue sales pressure in a person's home; and the use of harassment in debt recovery procedures.

If anyone suffers a loss as a result of any such breaches of the Act, legal advice should be sought, as a claim for damages may be possible through the Federal Court of Australia. Legal aid may be available for these actions through the Australian Legal Aid Office or from the Federal Attorney-General under section 170 of the Act.

Such actions can be very costly if legal aid is not available, and even if an order is obtained from the court there is no guarantee that certain fly-by-night companies will be found or have the funds to pay the damages awarded. Alternative remedies could be sought by joining an action already being taken by the Trade Practices Commission or by approaching the Department of Consumer Affairs to negotiate a settlement.

A recent amendment to the Act enables the Trade Practices Commission to apply to the court on behalf of consumers who have suffered loss or damage as a result of a breach of the consumer protection provisions of the Act. This means that consumers can take advantage of an action brought by the Commission, without the expense of taking a separate action themselves.

In addition to the protection already discussed, the Trade Practices Act provides specific rights to those defined as 'consumers' by the Act. Generally, a consumer is someone who has purchased goods or services from a company for less than $40,000; or where these goods or services are ordinarily obtained for personal, household or domestic use or consumption; or where the goods consist of commercial road vehicles.

This protection given to a consumer includes the right to be supplied with goods which are free from defects, and which are of 'merchantable' quality and fit for the purpose made known to the company before the purchase. There are also specific consumer rights in relation to the provision of services and to manufacturers and importers of goods.

When consumers wish to pursue their rights they are under an obligation to act as soon as possible. Their rights may include entitlement to a full refund as well as recovery of any losses incurred. These legal rights are in addition to any warranties or guarantees given by companies. The first step is to approach the company that supplied the goods in an assertive but non-aggressive manner. If the salesperson will not help, ask to see the manager. If this is unsuccessful, it may be appropriate to write to the manufacturer to claim compensation.

If these approaches do not work the Department of Consumer Affairs may negotiate a settlement on the consumer's behalf or refer the matter to the Small Claims Tribunal. As these tribunals only hear claims to a certain limit, it may necessary to seek legal advice from a legal centre or legal aid agency in order to pursue a claim in court.

A recent amendment to the Act prohibits unconscionable conduct by corporations in relation to the supply of goods or services ordinarily obtained for personal, domestic or household use or consumption. Where the court determines that a corporation has acted unconscionably it can order payment of compensation, refunds, injunctions, etc. An understanding of this section can also provide a useful negotiating tool to counsellors or others acting on behalf of consumers.

An essential resource for counsellors, which has been produced by the Trade Practices Commission, is titled *Shoppers Rights—A Guidebook on Consumers' Problems* Canberra: Australian Government Publishing Service, 1979. This booklet clearly and simply sets out the general consumer protection laws and individual consumer rights available under the Trade Practices Act. It considers how to go about obtaining these rights and there are many examples and important warnings to be noted by counsellors.

The Credit Acts

In broad terms, the Credit Acts give protection to consumers in the following ways:

- by providing a common system whereby consumers can shop for credit and compare the costs involved. This is brought about by regulating credit contracts, providing for more information in the advertising of credit and standardising the way interest rates are calculated.

- by setting up a system whereby consumers can understand their credit commitments by requiring that contracts be legible and that accurate information be given to consumers about their rights and responsibilities.

- by providing more equitable remedies for guarantors and debtors who are suffering from hardship.

- by requiring that lenders of regulated credit be licensed, and enabling the public to raise objections to the granting of licenses.

1. Regulated contracts

In general, credit contracts are regulated by the Acts if the amount borrowed is less than $20,000 and the interest rate is greater than 14 per cent. There are several exceptions, for example, in some states loans from co-operative societies, building societies, credit unions and pawnbrokers are not covered by the Credit Acts.

2. *Advertising*

The Acts prohibit 'false, misleading or deceptive' advertising of regulated credit. Also more information must be given in advertisements; for example, if a periodic payment of say $100 per month is shown, then the cash price of the goods or services, the total amount payable and the term of the loan must also be specified.

3. *Interest rates*

The confusing system whereby interest rates could be stated in terms of flat or effective rates has been replaced by an annual percentage rate. This means that consumers can readily compare the cost of credit and can refer to the legislation to find out how the interest is calculated.

4. *Written documents*

Documents covered by the Acts must be 'readily comprehensible'. Even the colour of the paper and the type of print must not detract from the legibility of the documents.

5. *Information given to credit recipients*

The Acts require lenders to provide certain information to borrowers, such as copies of credit contracts and notices which clearly explain the rights and responsibilities of borrowers. Failure to give specified information can result in the lender being prosecuted and the borrower being no longer liable to pay credit charges.

6. Guarantors

Guarantors of regulated credit are also provided with greater protection. They must be given notices setting out their rights and responsibilities as well as copies of guarantees and credit contracts. Also creditors must take specific steps before suing guarantors for payment of a debt. And if guarantors are unable to repay a debt as a result of hardship, they have certain rights to seek a variation of the contract.

7. Hardship provisions

If debtors are unable to maintain repayments as a result of hardship such as illness or unemployment, they can seek to have the credit contract varied when they can reasonably expect to maintain future repayments if this assistance is given.

8. Reopening of unjust contracts

If a regulated contract is unconscionable, harsh, oppressive or if the interest rate is excessive, relief can be granted by the Tribunal. The Credit Acts set out the circumstances to be considered in deciding whether a contract is unjust, for example, the intelligibility of the contract, whether expert advice was obtained and whether unfair pressure was used. The injustice must have been reasonably foreseeable at the time the contract or mortgage was entered into. Assistance may include setting aside or altering the contract, changing amounts owing under the contract and granting relief from payment.

9. Licensing of credit providers

The credit laws require that lenders of regulated credit must be licensed, although numerous organisations are exempted from the licensing provisions. Those exempted may include statutory authorities, banks, insurance companies, pawnbrokers, pastoral finance companies, cooperative societies, building societies and credit unions.

A licence can be refused by the licensing body on several

grounds which include the likelihood that the lender will not carry on their business 'honestly and fairly'. Once granted, licences can be suspended or cancelled if a credit provider contravenes the credit laws.

The Sale of Goods Acts

The Sale of Goods Act, 1923 (NSW), is an example of the type of consumer legislation which has been passed in the States and Territories throughout Australia. Unlike the Trade Practices Act, this State Act is not restricted to the sale of goods by corporations, but its application does have numerous limitations.

The Sale of Goods Act provides consumer rights and remedies in relation to contracts for the sale of goods but this does not include auction sales. Although these contracts include agreements to sell as well as actual sales, they do not include contracts for the supply of services. Contracts for the sale of goods can be made orally or in writing, or they can be implied by the parties' conduct, but there are certain requirements which must be complied with before these contracts can attract the provisions of the Act; for example, the contract must be of the value of $20 or more.

The main protection given to consumers is that certain conditions which are not expressly stated in these contracts of sale are implied by the Act. In general terms these implied conditions mean that the seller must have the right to sell the goods; if the goods are sold by description, they must fit the description; if the buyer makes known the purpose for which he wants the goods and relies on the seller's judgment, then the goods must be reasonably suitable for this purpose; and the goods must be of merchantable quality.

A breach of these conditions can mean that the buyer has the right to reject the goods and to sue for damages. Nevertheless it is usually preferable for the consumer to obtain a refund or replacement directly from the trader. If this is unsuccessful the buyer can contact the Department of Consumer Affairs, which may negotiate on the buyer's behalf or refer the matter to the Small Claims Tribunal. If the amount involved is outside the limit of the Tribunal, legal advice can be sought for an action to be taken to court.

Door-to-door sales legislation

The Door-to-Door Sales Act, 1967 (NSW), regulates the sale of goods and services which are sold by door-to-door salespeople. Many complaints received from consumers relate to contracts signed by people in their homes. It may be the case that a consumer signs a contract to buy unwanted items as a result of certain persuasive sales techniques, only to realise later that they cannot afford to pay for them. Under this Act consumers have the right to a ten-day cooling-off period and can cancel the contract and obtain a refund of any money paid. It is to be noted that the Act does not apply to cash sales or where the salesperson has attended the place or residence as a result of an unsolicited request by the consumer.

The Department of Consumer Affairs will assist people in relation to the Door-to-Door Sales Act as well as other important consumer legislation such as the Consumer Protection Act, 1969, Commercial Tribunal Act, 1984, Consumer Claims Tribunal Act, 1974, Contracts Review Act, 1980, Credit Act, 1984, Lay-by Sales Act, 1974, Motor Dealers Act, 1974, Pyramid Sales Act, 1974, Referral Selling Act, 1974, Textile Products Labelling Act, 1954, Unsolicited Goods And Services Act, 1974, and Weights And Measures Act, 1915.

Contracts Review Act, 1980 (NSW)

The Contracts Review Act enables the courts in New South Wales to give 'relief in respect of harsh, oppressive, unconscionable or unjust contracts'. The court may find such contracts or any part of a contract void. It may also vary the contract or refuse to enforce it. The Act sets out the circumstances which the court considers when determining whether a contract is unjust. These include whether there was any inequality in bargaining power between the parties, the literacy and educational background of the person seeking relief, the intelligibility of the contract and whether legal advice was sought. It is to be noted that the injustice must have been reasonably foreseeable when the parties entered into the contract.

The provisions of the Contracts Review Act can be a valuable tool to counsellors in negotiations. For example, to contact a credit provider on a client's behalf and declare that a certain term of a contract seriously offends one's social conscience is unlikely to achieve the desired response. On the other hand, to be able to refer to a certain section of the Act and show how the contract could be considered unjust will obviously carry more weight. The main advantage which a knowledge of this Act provides to a counsellor is to be able to find out when a referral for expert legal advice is appropriate for a client.

The law of contract

When these Commonwealth and State Acts do not apply to a particular situation, appropriate solutions may be found in the general law of contract. Contracts are made by people in their everyday lives when they buy goods and services. These contracts can be oral, written or implied by the conduct of the parties.

A financial counsellor must not simply accept that an agreement entered into by a client is necessarily a valid contract. It is therefore important to have at least a basic understanding of how a contract is formed, who can make a contract, what can constitute a breach of the contract, the difference between conditions and warranties, when a contract is void, voidable or unenforceable and the types of remedies available. The legal resource books referred to in the Introduction will be helpful here. For a more detailed text on contract law, see Cheshire and Fifoot *Law of Contract* Sydney: Butterworths, 1981.

Consumer resources

Consumer affairs departments in the various states and territories provide a wealth of information to inform consumers of their obligations, rights and remedies. The annual reports produced by these departments are useful sources of consumer information and provide details of investigations undertaken as well as the names of persons and companies convicted under the various acts administered by the departments.

The following is a guide to the information sheets, pamphlets and videos that can be obtained from the NSW Department of Consumer Affairs.

Pamphlets:

- *NSW Department of Consumer Affairs—What Does It Do For You?* sets out the reasons consumer protection is needed, the functions of the Department, how it helps consumers, the types of problems investigated by the Department and steps to be taken by consumers when making complaints about traders.

- *Rights of Consumers* explains what people can expect from the goods they purchase and provides information on how to buy, how to deal with salespeople and what to do if rights are violated.

- *Want to Complain About Goods or Services You've Bought?* outlines the steps to be taken by consumers in order to complain effectively about faulty goods.

- *Organisations Which Assist Consumers* provides the names, addresses, telephone numbers and a statement of functions of the State Government authorities, statutory boards, Federal Government organisations, private organisations and legal services which can aid consumers.

- *Consumer Credit Laws* is a set of seven pamphlets explaining the recent Credit Act, 1984 (NSW). The titles are self-explanatory:

Benefits for Consumers
Before You Sign Your Contract
After You Sign Your Contract
Worried About Repossession?
What About Insurance?
Going Guarantor?
Home Finance Contracts—Advice for Debtors and Guarantors
in Difficulty

- *Women Using Credit* discusses the types of problems experienced by women when applying for credit, important considerations prior to seeking credit, credit assessment factors used by lenders, how to overcome problems in obtaining credit, relevant provisions of the Credit Act, 1984, and steps to take if difficulties with repayments arise.

- *Buying a Car* considers the costs involved in buying a car, types of insurance cover, hints for purchasing new and used cars, consumer rights given by warranties and how to pursue these rights.

- *Door-to-Door Sales—Do's and Don'ts* advises consumers of the types of misleading statements used by disreputable salespeople and gives helpful suggestions to consumers for dealings with any door-to-door salespeople.

- *Lay-by Sales* answers several important questions in relation to consumer rights and obligations under the Lay-by Sales Act, 1943.

- *Textile Products Labelling* points out that consumers have 'the right to receive accurate information about a product so that a sensible buying decision can be made'. Such rights are protected by the Textile Products Labelling Act, 1954–70, and associated regulations, which are discussed in this pamphlet.

- *Date Stamping in New South Wales* provides comprehensive information on the date-stamping regulations introduced in 1978.

- *Packaging and Labelling Laws in New South Wales* lists the various Acts and regulations as well as the government departments and statutory bodies which regulate the labelling and packaging of food and other consumer products.

Printed information sheets include:

Background of the Department of Consumer Affairs

Acts and regulations administered by the Department of Consumer Affairs

Unordered goods

False and misleading advertising

Prices Commission of NSW

Pyramid selling

Referral selling

Inertia selling

Reduced 'sale' prices and offers to treat

NSW deceptive packaging legislation

Trade description (footwear) legislation

Care labelling

Weights and measures

Several of the pamphlets have been translated into various languages. Games and videos have also been produced by the Department.

Shopping skills

In the supermarket:

- Always prepare a list of the items required and keep to it. This will help control impulse buying.

- Go shopping as infrequently as possible. Extra trips to the supermarket usually mean that more money will be spent than intended.

- Avoid shopping when hungry as this will usually increase the food bill. It is hard to resist snack food and sweets which are so readily accessible when awaiting your turn at the checkout.

- Compare quality as well as price: simply because a product is cheaper does not mean it is more economical.

- Do not buy cans of food that are damaged: the contents could be affected.

- Check the date stamp on perishable items and on goods on 'special'.

- Watch weighing devices and cash registers: operators can make mistakes.

- Select a careful checkout operator, who calls the prices out aloud.

- Choose the supermarket that gives genuine specials, efficient service and good refrigeration.

Be aware:

- If you take your partner or children shopping with you, this will usually mean a substantial increase in the bill.

- It is fallacy that women are always better shoppers than men.

- Large packets of perishable food will be more expensive if not consumed.

- Meat, fruit and vegetables usually cost more in the supermarket than in the small specialist shops or at the markets.

- Displays are often moved around and staple food items placed at the rear of the store, which means that more items have to be viewed before finding the required item. This increases the temptation not to keep to the list.

- Confectionery is often placed on lower shelves within a child's reach.

- People often feel obliged to buy food if they are given a sample to taste.

- Specials are not always genuine: items can be marked as having been reduced when the prices have not actually changed.

- If two prices are marked on the item, the lower price must be charged.

- Price stickers are sometimes placed over expired 'use by' dates.

- There can be ingredients in food that you really do not want to consume. It is important to read the labels and avoid foods high in fat, sugar and salt.

- The most highly advertised and the most expensive items are not necessarily the best.

Other consumer goods:

- Shop around and compare quality, price, warranties, guarantees, after-sales service and availability of spare parts.

- Ask the opinion of family and friends who have bought similar items. For complex items, get the advice of an independent expert.

- Before buying goods make sure they are not faulty and that they fit the purpose for which you intend them.

- Make sure sales are genuine. Watch for 'going out of business sales', where the trader has been going out of business for years; 'fire sales', where the goods are sold at the usual retail price; or 'bait advertising', where you rush to a store after hearing an advertisement for a fabulous bargain only to find that they are all sold out, but that there is a similar item for a substantially higher price.

- Advertising has a major influence on what we buy. It is important to question why we want a particular product or a particular brand.

- A consumer always has the right to return defective goods, even if there are signs saying 'no refunds or exchanges accepted'. The purchaser does not have to accept a credit note instead of a cash refund.

- Receipts for major purchases should be kept in a safe place.

- Consumers do not have the right to a refund just because they change their mind.

- Nothing is for 'free'. The price of a 'gift' is often included in the cost of the item that has to be bought in order to obtain the gift.

Shoppers' resources

- The Australian Federation of Consumer Organisations Inc. produces a monthly magazine, *Consumer Views*, and has published useful booklets such as *A Pauper's Guide to Fast Food*.

- The Australian Consumers' Association publishes comparative tests of goods and services in its monthly magazine, *Choice*, and produces a quarterly issue titled *Consuming Interest*.

- The NSW Department of Health has prepared a booklet titled *How to Stretch the Food Dollar*, which includes hints on shopping and food storage as well as advice on good nutrition.

- Horan, Wall and Walker publish books of particular interest to shoppers such as *The Bargain Shopper's Guide to Sydney*, *Cheap Eats in Sydney* and *Cheap Plants and Gardens*.

3

The money plan

The money plan, or budget, is a key element in financial management and goes hand in hand with knowledge of consumer rights, shopping and cooking skills and wise investment planning. When people in our society experience financial problems they do have certain legal rights, but it is always better to prevent such difficulties than have to resort to legal remedies. One of the main ways in which financial problems can be avoided, or control of finances regained, is through the use of a money plan.

This simple life skill can help improve a person's standard of living, no matter how limited their resources, and thereby give them control over the financial predicament, rather than it having control over them. The money plan also helps to enhance self-esteem and to alleviate feelings of powerlessness because a person's needs and wants are more likely to be satisfied and goals are more readily achieved.

Money planning problems

You may well ask why more people do not make use of this valuable tool. The reasons are not hard to understand but the resistance can be difficult to overcome. It stems from people's very nature, from their life circumstances and from the various myths surrounding the money plan.

People erroneously believe that all that can help them is more money, that money planning is an enormous accounting effort or that it means living in a financial straitjacket. As a result, the very use of the word 'budget' is to be avoided because it raises such negative connotations.

It is easy to appreciate the negative reaction towards money planning of a person whose only source of income is a pension or benefit. The feeling can be 'what is the point anyway, when there is not even enough for basic necessities?'. It is well recognised that such an income does not provide for an adequate standard of living in our society, especially where the cost of housing is high. Nevertheless the fact remains that in practice where two people are in similar situations, the one who can plan their resources, make the best use of available facilities and gain control over their financial predicament will have the better standard of living. Money planning is not an answer to poverty but it can help alleviate the powerlessness that poverty creates.

When a person experiences a sudden and drastic reduction in income, for example, as a result of an injury causing permanent disabilities, the lifestyle adjustment is extremely difficult. It may be the case that a previously self-reliant person, through no fault of their own, finds themselves dependent on others and forced to change their whole way of life. There is not only the loss of health and employment to cope with but also the financial pressures of dependants, normal living expenses and credit commitments which can no longer be met.

In such a situation the resistance to money planning can be great because it means having to come to terms with drastic changes in lifestyle. Nevertheless there is little doubt that the sooner a person can regain control over their financial situation, the more readily they will be able to cope with all the associated traumas of such a crisis. It is very difficult for someone to work on the social and emotional aspects of a problem when they do not know where the next meal is coming from or whether it will be possible to keep a roof over the heads of their family.

Lack of communication about finances between family members is endemic in our society. Finances tend to be viewed in such a personal and private way that even a spouse can be left in the dark about the true financial state of affairs. As a result partners can be at cross-purposes over money matters.

One of the reasons for this problem is the lack of education about money management in our schools. It is well known that the younger a person is introduced to a concept in a positive way, the more readily it is accepted. Conversely, it is fairly basic to adult behaviour to reject what is not understood and to avoid change. Add to this a person's tendency to have unlimited wants, the easy access to expensive credit, the desire to 'keep up with the Joneses' and unrealistic expectations fuelled by advertising, and one has a basic formula for avoiding the money plan.

The breakdown in communication about finances means that partners' differing values, standards and goals come into conflict and certain myths about family money management are reinforced. Many people believe that financial skills are somehow inherent. Thus the husband is supposed to be able to handle the large expenses such as housing and the wife is expected to be able to take care of all the food and clothing costs. Such stereotyping leads to much distress and possibly even marital breakdown when expectations are not fulfilled and financial problems ensue.

Money planning can enhance family communication and help dispel the myths which inhibit the valuable use of family financial resources. It is the responsibility of the financial counsellor to recognise when money planning can assist a family or an individual, and to help them make and use such a plan. Most importantly, counsellors must practise what they preach. A counsellor who has never worked out their own money plan will have great difficulty in understanding the client's predicament.

How to make a money plan

1. The first step is for everyone in the family to take a note of what they spend each day for a period of at least two weeks. People often say 'I just don't know where my money has gone'. This exercise helps people find out where the gaps are in their spending, and there are usually many surprises. This is a valuable exercise for everyone so they can start to understand their own spending patterns and use it as a basis for discussion between family members.

2. The next step is to decide which expenditures are necessary, to put expenditures in order of priority and to decide short-term and long-term goals. If the money plan is for a family, it is important to include each member is this exercise in order to consider everyone's needs and wants. Unless this is done, compromises are not made and the plan can be frustrated because individual members are seeking to satisfy different objectives.

   The setting of goals is paramount in money planning as their achievement helps to reinforce the benefits and to motivate people to maintain the plan. Goals provide a light at the end of the tunnel.

   In the initial phase, it is sensible to set simple short-term goals. For example, for a single parent whose only source of income is a pension, a night out or a school excursion for the child can be realistic goals. Children can be very powerful in determining how money is to be spent. This can be tied in with the single parent's desire to make up for what they perceive the child is missing out on in some areas. Children can be quite clever in manipulating these feelings, for example, by insisting that all the other children in the class receive so much pocket-money each week. On the other hand, if children are involved in the planning of the family resources they can be incredibly understanding and supportive, and will learn an effective life skill.

   Read the Priorities Checklist on page 28 for some of the main expenditures people can have. It is a useful exercise to list these items in order of priority and decide which are absolute necessities, which items are wanted and which are not.

3. Add together net income from all sources coming into the household. This includes pensions, benefits, wages, family allowances, board and maintenance. Do not include unreliable sources of income such as irregular overtime and expected increases in earnings.

4. Use the Priorities Checklist to write down all expenses applicable to the individual or family and determine what each

PRIORITIES CHECKLIST

A Number each of the following items in order of priority:

Item	Number	Item	Number
Food	....	Transport	......
Clothing	....	Personal Expenses	......
Housing	....	Work Expenses	......
Utilities	....	Recreation	......
Medical Care	....	Gifts	......
Education	....	Credit Commitments	......

B For each of the following expenses write either 1 = necessary, 2 = would like to have or 3 = not wanted:

Food
groceries
(incs toiletries and
   cleansers) __
fruit and
   vegetables __
meat __
milk __
bread __
lunches away from
   home __
drinks __
pet food __
other __

Clothing
work __
school __
at home __
recreational __
underclothes __
shoes __
accessories __
cleaning __

Housing
rent or mortgage __
insurance (house &
   contents) __
rates (water &
   council) __
levies __
furniture __
carpets and
   curtains __

appliances __
maintenance __
garden supplies __

Utilities
electricity __
gas __
oil __
telephone __

Medical
doctor __
dentist __
chemist __
optometrist __
private health
   cover __

Education
fees __
books __
supplies __
excursions __

Transport
car __
   petrol __
   insurance __
   maintenance __
   registration __
   licence __
bus __
train __
taxi __

Personal
pocket-money __
life insurance __
haircuts __
cosmetics __

Work
union dues __
subscriptions __
equipment __
publications __

Recreation
newspapers, books
   and magazines __
movies __
dining out __
records __
pets __
equipment __
hobbies __
holidays __

Gifts
Christmas __
birthday __
other __

Credit
retail store credit __
credit sale contracts __
credit cards __
personal loans __
hiring charges __
other __

item costs. These expenses can be divided into categories which relate to the way money is allocated, for example:

(a) *Weekly cash expenses*: food, pocket-money, fares, petrol, school, newspapers, books, entertainment.

(b) *Regular bills*: rent, mortgage, rates, insurances, electricity, gas, telephone, car registration, licence, bankcard, charge account, personal loan, hiring charges.

(c) *Additional expenses*: clothing, medical, dental, optical, house maintenance, car maintenance, gifts, holidays.

5. Calculate the yearly cost of each item, then divide these by the number of pays each year to determine what amount needs to be set aside each pay. For example, if the pay day occurs weekly, divide the yearly amount by 52 and if it occurs fortnightly then divide the yearly amount by 26. It is necessary for calculations to be accurate, otherwise insufficent amounts will frustrate the plan. For example, a weekly rental of $100 is to be multiplied by 52 to arrive at the yearly amount and then divided by the pay period. If the income is received monthly then the calculation is $100 \times 52 \div 12 = $433 per month. If the weekly rental had simply been multiplied by four the money plan would be short by $33 per month. This amount can make a large difference to a family on a low income.

6. The final step is to total all expenses and subtract these from the net income. The difference will be the amount put into savings for the achievement of goals.

How to use a money plan

1. If there are no savings, priorities must be reconsidered and this will mean reducing expenses or increasing income.

2. When the cash is set aside for weekly expenses, it is important to determine who manages the money and to ensure that it is only spent on the items for which it has been allocated. Remember that social stereotypes can be dysfunctional. For

example, it is not always the woman who is the better grocery shopper.

3. A simple and convenient savings plan will improve the money plan because it will bring peace of mind to know that the money is there to pay the bills and to know that the achievement of goals is at hand. Some people find it helpful to place the money for their regular bills in a special bill-paying account, the money for additional expenses in a separate account and then an account for their goals. Of course if there is a large surplus, it is important to shop around for safe, professional investment advice.

4. When a money plan is first set up there may be frustrations when a large expense occurs for which sufficient sums have not as yet accumulated. It may take almost a year for a bill-paying account to be fully effective. The person may need encouragement to continue, so point out that the aim of the money plan is to have the money for all such future expenses.

5. Although making a money plan may take a few hours, after that it is simply a matter of allocating the income each pay day. It also helps to occasionally keep a record of expenditure for a couple of weeks to check it against the plan.

6. The money plan cannot be a straitjacket. It must be flexible or it will not be maintained. As the needs and circumstances of people change, so must the money plan. Updating is also necessary to keep up with rising costs, especially if an allowance is not made within the money plan for inflation.

7. The money plan must be tailored to suit the needs of each individual or family. See page 31 for an example of such a money plan.

Advantages

The reason for money planning is the many advantages which result from its implementation. These include:

MONEY PLAN

Net Income

	Per Pay Period (Wk, F' night, Mth)
Wages	$.............
Pension or benefit	$.............
Family allowance	$.............
Board	$.............
Other	$.............
Total income	$_____

Cash Expenses

	Per Year	Per Pay Period
Food (meat, veg, groceries)	$.............	$.............
Pocket-money	$.............	$.............
Fares	$.............	$.............
Petrol	$.............	$.............
School	$.............	$.............
Newspapers, magazines	$.............	$.............
Entertainment (alcohol, cigs)	$.............	$.............
Other	$.............	$.............
1. Total cash from income		$_____

Regular Bills

	Per Year	Per Pay Period
Rent/mortgage	$.............	$.............
Rates (council & water)	$.............	$.............
Insurances (house, contents, life, car)	$.............	$.............
Electricity, gas, oil	$.............	$.............
Telephone	$.............	$.............
Car (registration, licence)	$.............	$.............
Bankcard/s	$.............	$.............
Charge account/s	$.............	$.............
Personal loan/s	$.............	$.............
Rental/s	$.............	$.............
2. Total in bill-paying account		$_____

Additional Expenses

	Per Year	Per Pay Period
Clothing	$.............	$.............
Medical	$.............	$.............
Dental	$.............	$.............
House maintenance	$.............	$.............
Car maintenance	$.............	$.............
Gifts	$.............	$.............
Holidays	$.............	$.............
Other	$.............	$.............
3. Total in expenses account		$_____

Total Income	$_____
Total Expenses (1 + 2 + 3)	$_____
Surplus in goal account	$_____

- the saving of time, money and stress;

- making the best use of limited financial resources;

- having the peace of mind that comes with good money management;

- the improvement of living standards when used in conjunction with other life skills;

- prevention of impulse buying and overcommitment, when this is due to inadequate planning;

- helping to sort out financial priorities and the achievement of goals;

- enhancement of family communication;

- providing for financial support in an emergency and security in retirement;

- keeping records, which is a great help at tax time.

Ingredients

A money plan must have PIP: the Positive, Individual and Practical ingredients which make a money plan work.

The *positive* aspects of the money plan are the many advantages gained from using this life skill. Pointing out these advantages will help to overcome the resistance to money planning, and the practising of this skill by the counsellor will help to share hints and appreciate hurdles. The plan will become more positive if it is shared by all members of the family and communication will be enhanced.

Unless a money plan is straightforward and *individual*, confidence can be lost, resulting in the plan being aborted. When money plans are complex with more headings than are needed, frustration and anger can be felt when the person is unable to afford all the expenses listed. The individualisation of the money plan also shows an appreciation of the person's special needs and circumstances.

People may be carried away at the beginning of a money plan and want to make drastic changes to their spending patterns. For example, a fast food addict may decide to turn vegetarian overnight. When such impractical decisions do not work, the money plan stops. It is more *practical* to start with achievable goals and simple skills, such as the improvement of shopping skills. Although many people believe they can do money planning in their heads, the most successful and practical money plans are those that are written.

4

Loans and the way they work

In our materially oriented society the availability of credit enables consumers to obtain the goods and services they need and want without having to save for them. This has meant not only that more goods have been able to be produced and purchased but also that an increasingly sophisticated and varied system of providing credit has developed to accommodate the increasing demands of consumers.

The laws which have developed to regulate this system of credit have generally not kept pace with the constantly growing and changing credit industry. Also the complexity and variety of credit legislation and the lack of uniformity between the laws of the states and territories have made the education of consumers an increasingly difficult task.

Those that suffer most in such a system tend to be those most in need. Not only do the poor pay more for credit but they are the least likely to have an understanding of the system or be aware of their rights.

There is pressing need for governments to provide low interest consumer loans for low income earners and for schools to educate children about their rights and responsibilities as future users of credit. It is also the responsibility of those in the helping professions, who have the most contact with the more 'vulnerable' consumers, to have an understanding of our credit system so that appropriate assistance and referrals can be provided.

What is credit?

Credit occurs when you borrow cash or are given extended time to pay for goods and services. There is usually a charge for the use of credit, known as interest, and there can be associated costs such as stamp duty, legal expenses and application fees.

Therefore buying on credit involves paying for the cash, goods or services as well as for the use of the credit.

Advantages of credit

Because counsellors are continually confronted with the problems that arise with the use of credit, it is very easy to develop a 'siege mentality'. It is therefore important to maintain a balanced perspective and consider the many advantages of credit.

Credit enables people to:

- purchase major items such as a house or car, which can substantially increase a person's standard of living and which would be impossible to obtain without the availability of credit;

- have the use of goods and services while still paying for them;

- obtain funds to start and develop a business;

- have the ability to obtain cash for emergencies;

- acquire necessary household items and clothing;

- save money by purchasing goods on sale when sufficient cash is not available (but the cost of the credit must be added to the sale price to determine the actual cost of the goods);

- even obtain goods without having the ready cash and not be charged for the use of the credit, when certain credit facilities are used wisely;

- shop without having to carry large sums of money.

Credit assessment

Throughout this book, the perspective of the consumer is considered. This section however attempts to look at the way a credit provider views the world.

The most interesting concept is that the people who process credit transactions tend to think that they are lending their own money, not someone else's, and this probably reflects the training programs they go through. But this raises a very important point. They are lending someone else's money, that of their depositors and shareholders. As they are accountable to these people in the long run, they therefore either tend to make decisions that are extremely profitable or extremely conservative.

It is useful then to try to look at the process that credit providers should go through (and reputable credit providers do) in assessing a credit transaction. They would consider:

- a borrower's profile, indicating whether the person is a good credit risk;

- the person's ability to repay;

- the security that can be offered to make their loan decision rest easier;

- economic and other conditions imposed to protect the credit provider from loss.

1. The borrower's profile

The cliché is as true today as it was many years ago: 'honesty is the best policy'. With sophisticated checking mechanisms available, the credit provider can detect most attempts to state incorrect information. The answer to attempts to paint a better-than-real picture is, at very least, to view the application with a great deal of suspicion. It probably means that the loan will be declined. It is also noteworthy that credit providers ask the borrower to sign a declaration of honesty on the application form. Depending upon the nature of any incorrect information stated in the application form, a credit provider can and sometimes does look at legal action for attempted fraud and similar issues of law.

These are the areas that are looked at in an attempt to build up a picture of the borrower:

(a) *Stability.* According to financiers the longer people have lived in one place and worked at one job, the more likely they are to be citizens who will honour commitments. This concept has been a basic consideration of providers of credit for as long as most can remember, although this may be changing a little these days.

(b) *Track record.* While the previous concept is subjective, this concept is based on reported history. If a borrower has made repayments on time and has had no recorded problems with credit in the past, all things being equal, he or she is considered to be a good risk.

This of course raises a number of problems. What if this is the first time the borrower has applied for credit? The borrower may have never worked before or may have always paid cash for items in the past. When a track record is not readily available it is common for credit providers to seek security or a guarantor for the loan.

(c) *Other factors.* Depending upon family or other connections with a lender, smaller loans may be granted where otherwise questions may have been asked. It probably boils down to who you know rather than what you know. This would normally happen when someone with whom the borrower has this type of understanding has an approval limit and exercises their own discretion. For many years there has been another concept: get to know your bank manager. A borrower may have more of a chance of success if the request is reasonable and well presented, and the borrower is a name not just a number.

The other purely subjective judgments revolve around the borrower's marital status, number of children and type of work. Most credit providers would therefore agree that a married professional person with children is a better risk than a single process worker. The author's assertion is that such matters in themselves are not relevant. But depending upon the size of the loan, the risk can be evaluated by knowing more about the person borrowing. The sad reality is that in today's pressured society being a number on a computer is more the reality than would be preferred.

2. *Ability to repay*

Perhaps this is the most confusing and misunderstood area in the credit decision. Yet it really should be the easiest. Many credit providers use the rule of thumb that the amount to be repaid must not exceed a stipulated percentage of gross income; others say that a borrower will spend an amount that has been calculated on the basis of family size and income. In other words no matter which way you look at it, the borrower is generally stereotyped and classified.

Why have credit providers adopted this attitude? Simply because they believe that most borrowers are their own worst enemies. In many instances they are proven correct when they see the persuasive salesmen convince us that we really need the product they are paid to sell us, or our expectations in life are such that we are not prepared to wait to realise them.

It is important that borrowers know what they can afford and be able to realistically appraise the proposition. When those in the helping professions and educators generally learn these simple skills, they can pass this knowledge on to their clients with confidence, and help them to prevent the problems that can arise with the uninformed use of credit.

3. *Security for the loan*

There are several forms of 'security' that a lender has in the transaction. The first of these is the amount of deposit that can be provided towards any purchase that may be financed. The greater the amount of deposit, the 'safer' the person is as a borrower.

More formal security consists of mortgages and other securities which may be required to be executed in the lender's favour, usually because of the size of the loan or an unproven track record. The main point to remember here is that should default occur and repossession procedures be set in motion, the security will be sold to repay the debt. Or in the case of a guarantor, legal action may be initiated against a third party to ensure that the borrower honours the obligation to the lender. Suffice to say that all these matters bear the most detailed consideration, even though credit legislation in some states regulates the way this is done and sets out borrowers' rights on these issues.

As with all issues in this book, it is essential that clients experiencing problems in this area receive expert advice on their position. All documentation entered into must be supplied to the legal adviser or financial counsellor so that an accurate assessment of the position can be made at the time.

4. *Other conditions of the loan*

Aside from economic conditions which may determine the amount of money available to lend because of interest rates etc., there are other conditions that lenders may impose on a borrower to ensure that the lender's position of safety is maintained. For example, they may insist that the goods which are the subject of the security be insured and safeguarded at all times. Or it may be a requirement that the goods not be used for any purpose that their manufacturer had not intended them to be used for.

The point of this is that all conditions of any loan must be spelt out in the contract that was signed at the time of the loan being made available. Any conditions not included in this loan contract cannot be subsequently added. Clients must read and understand the contents of any contract that they sign. Many people feel intimidated: unless they sign immediately, they don't get the loan. The point is that having signed the contract, it is much more difficult, though not impossible, to get around the situation later on. Without question the important message is not to sign any document that contains clauses that are not understood or agreed with. This is especially so in the area of special conditions imposed outside the usual contract.

The credit reference system

The most widely used system for checking the credit worthiness of borrowers in Australia is through the Credit Reference Association (CRA). This Association is a co-operative-type organisation owned by its members, which include finance companies, banks, building societies, credit unions and department stores.

CRA uses a highly computerised system which at present holds information on approximately five million consumers throughout Australia. This information includes names, addresses, employment details, birth dates, drivers' licence numbers, credit enquiries, defaults, legal action and bankruptcies. The details are obtained from credit providers and public records.

When a consumer applies for credit through a member of the Association, a credit check will usually be made. If the prospective borrower has previously applied for credit within a certain time, a record of his or her credit history will be available.

This record will give the borrower's particulars and any requests for credit will be shown. These enquiries state the name of the lender, the date of the enquiry, the amount applied for and the type of account. It does not indicate whether the application for credit was approved; such information must be obtained from the relevant credit provider.

If the borrower has not kept up repayments on previous credit commitments, defaults may be noted on the file as well as certain legal actions, such as a judgment or bankruptcy.

The information on a borrower's CRA file shows a credit history rather than a credit rating. These details are retained for a maximum of five years, except for a bankruptcy, which is deleted after seven years.

If borrowers are denied credit as a result of an incorrect CRA file, they can have the error corrected by advising the Association. If any difficulties arise, the matter can be referred to the Privacy Commission for consideration.

Usually spouses are shown as joint borrowers and have the same credit history. If a couple separate or divorce they can make an application to CRA for a separate credit file. But the files will be subsequently linked if joint accounts are again entered into by the couple.

Anyone can apply for a copy of their credit file by contacting CRA and paying a fee of five dollars. If a person has been refused credit in the previous month, there is no charge for a copy of the CRA file.

The Credit Reference Association plays an important part in our system of credit and helps in preventing overcommitment which can arise with the ready availability of consumer credit. The need for this prevention particularly occurs in the case of the 'compulsive' borrower, who continues to borrow regardless of inability to repay. This dysfunctional behaviour is usually the result of underlying psychological or emotional problems, which are only exacerbated by the pressure of not being able to repay debts.

Types of credit

The most common types of consumer credit are personal loans, retail store credit, credit cards, overdrafts and hire-purchase.

1. Personal loans

Personal loans are loans of cash, which can be obtained from banks, building societies, credit unions and finance companies. These loans can be taken for any number of needs: to buy a car, household goods or pay for a holiday.

An advantage of a personal loan is that substantial savings can be obtained by shopping around to borrow cash for the goods required, rather than simply accepting credit from the supplier of the goods. A common example is the purchase of a car, where a borrower can save many hundreds of dollars in interest by obtaining a personal loan from a bank or credit union rather than accepting the credit offered by the car dealer.

Personal loans can be secured or unsecured. The higher the amount borrowed and the greater the credit risk, the more likely it is that the loan will be secured. A secured loan means that the borrower has given certain goods or land as surety for the loan.

The borrower still owns the property but cannot sell it without the lender's consent. Security is usually taken in the form of a bill of sale or a mortgage, and these documents must be registered. If a borrower defaults in repaying the secured loan, the lender can repossess and sell the goods or land. In most cases where the sale proceeds do not fully cover the outstanding debt, the lender can take further legal action to recover the balance of the loan. This further legal action cannot be taken if the loan is regulated by the Moneylending Act (NSW) and is secured by a bill of sale.

2. Retail store credit

Retail store credit cards are mainly available from the large department stores which issue these cards to eligible customers. These charge accounts enable customers to purchase any item for sale in the store up to a specified limit.

When goods are sold on these terms, the purchaser owns the goods and the store has no further claim on these items. If the customer defaults in repaying the account, the store cannot repossess the goods but can enforce the debt through the courts.

The main advantage of retail store credit is that there is usually no charge for the use of credit if the account is paid in full within the billing cycle. This usually gives the customer at least 30 days in which to pay for the goods without any interest charges. If used wisely, up to 60 days interest-free credit can be obtained by making purchases immediately after the closing date of the account. The annual percentage rates charged on department store accounts vary greatly and are calculated on the average daily balance outstanding from the end of the previous billing cycle.

3. Credit cards

The type and number of credit cards is ever increasing. These revolving credit facilities include Bankcard, Visa Card and Master Card. Credit cards enable consumers to continually borrow up to a fixed limit and can be used to buy goods and services at a variety of outlets. The versatility and ready availability of credit cards have made them one of the most widely used forms of credit in Australia.

The annual percentages rates charged on credit cards also vary and, as in the case of department store accounts, most credit cards allow for interest-free purchases if the total account is paid within the billing cycle, usually 30 days. Again the maximum benefit can be obtained by charging purchases to the account directly after the closing date. For example, an interest-free period of up to 55 days can be achieved by using Bankcard this way.

Consumers are often unaware that on cards which allow for cash advances, interest is charged at a daily rate from the date of the cash advance. This can be a very expensive way of obtaining ready cash, but can also be cheaper than borrowing from lending institutions that charge ever higher rates of interest.

When purchases are made with these cards, the supplier of the goods and services bills the credit card company, which in turn bills the consumer. Consumers can be billed incorrectly and it is important to keep receipts and check these against the statement of account. If the credit card is regulated by the Credit Act (NSW), the borrower has two billing cycles from the date of the lender's reply in which to have any error rectified. After this period the lender can take legal action to recover any outstanding repayments.

4. Overdrafts

Overdraft facilities through banks enable customers to withdraw more funds than are available in their accounts. Overdrafts are usually only available to long-term customers and are normally secured by an interest-bearing deposit account or some other security. Overdrafts are made available through cheque account facilities and borrowers pay stamp duty on each cheque as well as interest on the amount overdrawn. Other charges can include state and federal duties, account-keeping charges and service fees.

5. Hire-purchase

Until recently hire-purchase was one of the most widely used forms of consumer credit, especially in relation to purchase of motor vehicles. In New South Wales, Western Australia, Victoria and the ACT hire-purchase has been dispensed with by the Credit Acts. Nevertheless there are still many current hire-purchase contracts which were entered into before the introduction of the Credit Acts, and it is necessary for counsellors to understand consumers' rights and responsibilities in relation to these contracts.

A hire-purchase agreement enables the borrower to hire goods from the supplier of the credit, and ownership of the goods passes to the borrower when the final instalment is paid. The Hire Purchase Acts provide protection to consumers who enter into these agreements. For example, the Hire Purchase Act, 1960 (NSW), provides the following consumer rights:

- Hire-purchase agreements must be in writing and signed by all parties to the agreement.

- Before signing the agreement the hirer must be given a First Schedule notice which provides the details of the cost of entering into the contract. The information includes the cash price of the goods, a description of the goods, the amount of the deposit, instalment details, terms charges and the total amount payable.

- Once the contract has been signed, a copy of the agreement and a statement of the hirer's rights must be given to the hirer within 21 days of entering the hire-purchase agreement.

- If a hirer does not maintain repayments, the owner can repossess the goods but, in most cases, a Third Schedule notice must be issued 21 days before repossession. This notice informs the hirer of the owner's intention to repossess and advises the amount of the arrears.

- If goods are repossessed, a Fourth Schedule notice must be served on the hirer. The goods cannot be sold within 21 days of this notice which explains how the hirer can regain the goods, and if this is not possible, the hirer's refund or liability.

- Although the owner has the right to insist that the hirer insure the goods which are subject to the agreement, the hirer has the right to choose his own insurance company. This can mean a substantial saving to a hirer who shops around for insurance.

- A hirer has the right to terminate the agreement at any time by informing the owner in writing and paying the 'net balance due' under the agreement. In most cases, if repayments can no longer be met, it is preferable for the hirer to obtain the owner's permission to sell the goods privately rather than returning them to the owner. For example, in the case of a car, the hirer often obtains a better price selling privately than the owner (usually a finance company) would obtain at auction.

- If the owner does not comply with certain provisions of the Act, rights to the interest payments and sometimes the balance outstanding may be forfeited.

The general principles of the Hire-Purchase Acts throughout Australia are similar although the operation of the Acts in the various states differs in detail. It is therefore necessary for counsellors to familiarise themselves with the legislation in their state in order to be able to help clients with these agreements.

The Credit Acts

The Credit Acts which were implemented in Western Australia, Victoria, New South Wales and the ACT in 1985 replaced some of the legislation which had previously regulated the provision of credit, including the Hire-Purchase Acts and the Money Lenders Acts. As a result, there now exists a dual system whereby contracts entered into before the start of the Credit Acts are still regulated by the old laws and counsellors must understand the rights and remedies provided by both systems. This confusion is exacerbated by the fact that although the Credit Acts are generally uniform, certain provisions and in particular the regulations do vary between the states.

Most provisions of the NSW Credit Act came into force on 28 February 1985. In general credit in New South Wales is regulated by the Act if the amount borrowed is less than $20,000 and the annual percentage rate is greater than 14 per cent. Exceptions to this include loans from credit unions and building societies.

The Act provides for three forms of credit contracts. These are 'credit sale contracts', 'loan contracts' and 'continuing credit contracts'.

1. Credit sale contracts

Credit sale contracts are contracts for goods or services where:

(a) the cash price does not exceed $20,000 (or where the goods include farm machinery or commercial vehicles);
(b) the supplier of the goods or services also provides the credit; and
(c) a charge is made for the credit.

A typical credit sale contract occurs where a consumer buys a car from a dealer, who also provides the finance for the car. Many loans of this type were previously taken out as hire-purchase agreements.

2. Loan contracts

Generally loan contracts are regulated by the Act where:

(a) the amount of the loan does not exceed $20,000 and the annual percentage rate is greater than 14 per cent; and
(b) one or more of the following apply:
- a sum of money is paid to the debtor;
- there is a reduction, variation or deferment of a debt;
- a bill of exchange or other negotiable instrument is taken from a debtor.

A common example of a loan contract is a loan of money from

a finance company which can be used for any purpose, such as a holiday or to purchase consumer goods.

The Act provides specific protection to consumers who enter into credit sale and loan contracts. In certain circumstances, the credit provider may be subject to prosecution and the debtor relieved of any liability to pay the credit charges under the contract if:

● the contract is not in writing;

● certain disclosures are not made in the contract, such as details of the amount financed, the credit charges, the annual percentage rate, to whom and where payments are to be made and any commission payable;

● any mortgage relating to the contract is not in writing.

Further protections relate to the comprehensibility of the contracts, notices of the rights and obligations of the borrower which must be provided within 14 days of entering the contract, and the obligation of the creditor to provide copies of contracts, notices, insurance and mortgage documents within a specified time. A credit provider can only vary a credit sale or loan contract if seven days' notice is given to the debtor and the contract provides for such a variation.

3. Continuing credit

Continuing credit occurs if the borrower can obtain credit 'from time to time' for the supply of cash, goods or services. Generally contracts are regulated by the Act if the annual percentage rate is greater than 14 per cent and the amount borrowed is less than $20,000. Continuing credit contracts include Bankcards, Visa Cards and retail store credit cards.

The Act gives certain rights to borrowers of continuing credit. Before a debt is incurred the borrower must receive a statement setting out his or her rights and responsibilities, and a notice which includes details about the contract. Also statements of account must, in most cases, be provided eight days before the end of the billing cycle and must include specified information.

If a debtor reasonably believes a billing error has occurred, this can be queried in writing before the payment is due. Such action means that the credit provider cannot enforce the debt for two complete billing cycles after advising the debtor of any decision. If the debtor finds the decision unsatisfactory, an application for determination can be made to the Commercial Tribunal before the end of the two billing cycles.

Counsellors need to study in detail the Credit Act and regulations relevant to their particular state or territory in order to be able to give appropriate advice on credit.

Important terms

Guarantors

When someone applies for credit, the lender may require that the prospective borrower obtain a guarantor for the loan. Usually this will occur when a person has no long-term employment record or credit history. Typically an 18-year-old applying for finance to buy a car will be asked to have someone guarantee the loan; this will most likely be a parent.

Becoming a guarantor means that if the borrower does not maintain repayments, the lender can pursue the guarantor for any arrears. This can be a cause of real hardship for the guarantor. For example, if a parent, whose only source of income is a pension and only asset is the family home, becomes guarantor for a son or daughter who can no longer maintain the debt, there is the possibility of the creditor taking possession of the house to recover the amount owing.

The Credit Acts provide certain protection to guarantors of regulated credit:

- A credit provider cannot enforce a contract of guarantee unless it is in writing, signed by the guarantor and a copy of the debtor's contract is provided before the guarantee is signed.

- Within 14 days of signing the contract of guarantee, a copy must be received by the guarantor as well as a statement of rights and obligations under the Act.

● If a credit provider wants to recover an amount from the guarantor, he must bring proceedings against both the debtor and guarantor or obtain judgment against the debtor and wait 30 days after a letter of demand. In certain circumstances the guarantor can be sued first alone, for example, if the debtor cannot be found or a court decides it unlikely that the debtor can pay any part of the debt.

● If as a result of 'illness, unemployment or other reasonable cause' the guarantor is unable to pay the creditor, an application can be made to vary the contract. If the creditor does not agree to an arrangement, the guarantor can seek assistance from the Department of Consumer Affairs.

Co-borrowers

A co-borrower is jointly and severally liable for the debt and has fewer protections than a guarantor. Either or both borrowers can be called on to pay the debt and it is therefore to the lender's advantage to have co-borrowers rather than guarantors. This practice appears to have increased since the introduction of the Credit Acts, which have made it more difficult for the credit provider to recover the debt from the guarantor.

Joint tenants and tenants in common

When land is purchased by two or more people it is necessary to decide whether the title is to be held by them as joint tenants or tenants in common.

Joint tenancies can only be created at the outset of the purchase of the property. It is the most commonly favoured tenancy between spouses because it means that if one partner dies the survivor becomes the sole owner of the property regardless of any will. Alternatively, if two or more people hold the property as tenants in common and one of the owners dies, his or her share will be distributed according to a will or the laws of intestacy.

Ignorance of these terms can lead to disastrous results. For example, two friends, Jane and Pam, buy a property, and unwittingly become tenants in common. One friend, Jane, has saved all the money for the deposit, thus enabling the purchase of the house. Not long after moving into the new house, the friend, Pam, dies in a car accident. Even if the girls intended that the house would become the property of the surviving joint owner this would not occur unless stated in Pam's will. It is often the case that people have not made wills, and in this situation, Jane would lose half of the property to Pam's next of kin, who may require the property to be sold in order to obtain the money from the half-share of the house.

It is my experience that very few people who buy property together know whether it is held as joint tenants or tenants in common. It is essential that a counsellor be able to explain these terms and explain the importance of making a will.

Hints for using credit

- Ensure that you can afford the credit. Make a money plan and on each pay day place an amount equivalent to the loan repayment in a savings account. This will help you save for a deposit and enable you to determine whether you can afford the repayments.

- The more you save for a deposit, the less the credit will cost. Never borrow the deposit.

- The cost of the credit will be significantly reduced by repaying the loan over as short a period as possible.

- Shop around for credit. Interest rates vary greatly and significant savings can be made by comparing various sources of credit.

- Add together the total costs of obtaining credit to decide whether the expense is worth while. Costs can include interest, stamp duty, application fees, legal costs, establishment fees and insurances. Other expenses involved in the purchase must also be considered, such as servicing, maintenance, registration and depreciation.

- Do not sign the contract unless you fully understand the terms, and ensure that there are no blank spaces.

- Read any notices you receive about your rights and responsibilities under the contract and keep these with the contract in a safe place.

- Make sure the goods you are purchasing will fit the purpose for which you are buying them. In general you cannot change your mind about a credit contract simply because you later discover the items you bought were the wrong colour or size.

- If the goods you buy on credit are secured by a mortgage and must be insured, shop around for insurance. Do not automatically accept the insurance offered by the credit provider. Remember that when an insurance premium is included in the loan contract, interest is charged on this amount.

- Consider taking out insurance to cover the repayments, at least on major credit commitments, in the event of crises such as illness, unemployment or death. But ensure you understand the type of insurance you are taking out, as terms can be confusing. For example, many people confuse mortgage guarantee and mortgage protection insurances. This can cause great hardship when people erroneously believe they have a life cover when paying for mortgage guarantee insurance on a home loan. Mortgage guarantee insurance only protects the *lender* if the consumer defaults, if the mortgaged property is sold, and if an insufficient amount is realised to pay the debt in full.

- Find out the penalties and your responsibilities if you cannot maintain repayments, and what happens if you wish to increase repayments or pay out the contract before the end of the loan term.

- Substantial savings may be possible if loans can be paid off early.

5

Techniques of financial counselling

Casework forms the basis of all the work done by financial counsellors. The main aim of the counselling interview is to understand the cause of the problem so that appropriate alternatives can be developed. It is then that the educational and skill development aspects of financial counselling can be put into practice. The casework also provides the necessary data for effecting change, such as in the area of legislative reform.

The underlying causes of a client's difficulties can involve a combination of social, emotional, psychological, physical and financial factors. The complex and often indivisible nature of these factors requires that the counsellor employ all the elements of effective communication and appropriate interviewing techniques. It is not within the scope of this book to present the knowledge and skills that can only be learnt in counselling courses and experience in the field. But I would like to highlight some of the most necessary elements of the financial counselling interview. These include developing trust and spending time.

Time

A financial counsellor must be willing to invest time in resolving the problem with the client. Not only will the initial interview normally take at least two hours, but generally there will be subsequent interviews and much follow-up work in the form of negotiating, letter-writing and liaising with relevant welfare and government bodies.

Time is an investment of ourselves, and cues about our commitment to the client will be apparent from the outset. Obvious factors include the prompt way a client is greeted, ensuring that the interview is not interrupted by telephone calls, and clearing the desk beforehand to show that your time is for that person.

Appropriate timing within the interview is a vital and more difficult skill. Although the very nature of a financial counselling interview calls for a directive approach this should not be confused with the skirting of important issues in order to get to the dollars and cents. Rushing through the social and emotional aspects of the problem will rapidly shut down communication and inhibit the level of objectivity needed by the client to make appropriate financial decisions. The depth to which these issues can be canvassed will depend on the skill of the counsellor.

It is not the role of the financial counsellor to provide psychological, marital or bereavement counselling, but it is necessary to discover when these referrals are required. Unless the whole person is dealt with, the financial problem is unlikely to be resolved.

The investment of our time will also promote the development of the trust necessary to achieve the goal of the casework.

Trust

Most people, even when they are not experiencing problems, consider their financial affairs to be a very private matter which they may not even discuss with those closest to them. When financial difficulties arise accompanied by emotions of fear, pride, anger and loss, it can be an even greater imposition to have to disclose financial details.

It is therefore essential to open up lines of communication by establishing a trusting relationship at the outset. In the initial stages of an interview trust can be promoted by passive listening. This involves the judicious use of silence and appropriate non-verbal communication. By allowing the client to speak and not jumping in to fill uncomfortable gaps in the conversation, much can be learnt from the client. We let the client know that we understand and care about what they are saying by nodding, maintaining eye contact and other appropriate visual responses.

The development of trust requires that the counsellor be non-judgmental and accepting of the client. In our society we are brought up to be critical of people whose lives are not working and to judge them by our own values and ideas of what is 'right'. Such a critical attitude will be betrayed in the counsellor's tone of voice and through verbal and non-verbal communication. The very words we use can be blaming, critical and antagonistic. Phrases such as 'You should. . .', 'You make me. . .', 'You always. . .' arouse defensiveness and quickly close down communication. If we accept the client, without blaming, criticising or psychoanalysing, trust will rapidly be established.

A powerful tool in establishing trust is 'active' listening. The content of what a client says can be misleading or inaccurate because it is just too painful to get down to what the problem is really about. If the emotions underlying the words can be accurately reflected back to the client, then the person will feel not just listened to but really heard and may then be willing to go deeper into the problem.

For example, I might see a man who has been unemployed for many months and is about to lose his home for non-payment of the mortgage. This is a devastating situation for any person, especially one who is accustomed to being the provider in the family. He may be feeling angry at the system and ashamed in front of his family for not being able to provide for them. If I am accurately reflecting his despair by saying: 'It must be really painful for a man like you who is accustomed to being the provider of the family', then he may be prepared to express his anger and pain and go deeper into the problem.

Until a person has had an opportunity to express emotions, there will be blind spots which will inhibit relating on a rational level. Once these feelings have been released, the person can move on to the problem-solving stage and more readily work with the counsellor to develop solutions.

The directive approach

A financial counselling interview requires a directive approach in order to find out all the information necessary to develop viable alternatives. This would mean clarifying the client's expectations at the start of the interview and explaining what the service offers.

To help in maintaining the focus of the interview a structure which is acceptable to the client is outlined. For instance, I might say: 'What I would like to do today is gain an understanding of your difficulties, consider your financial position and look at the alternatives available to you'. In this way the client is given notice of what is involved in the interview and will feel more comfortable with the process.

Throughout the interview the directive approach will mean that issues are confronted and clarified. The counsellor must ascertain facts, which means facing the problems with the client, and to admitting to the client anything that is not understood.

The facts will be clarified by repeating key words, summarising what the client has said and using 'open-ended questions'. These questions cannot be answered with a simple yes or no. They begin with words like 'how', 'when', 'what' and 'who'. By offering very probing questions such as, 'How do you feel about that?' or 'What do you want to do?' you not only obtain necessary information but help to bring the client to their own solutions.

The financial position

Although no two interviews will be the same, a general pattern can be seen. When the social and emotional issues have been appropriately explored and the facts of the situation clarified, the financial position can then be considered. Of course it may happen that further facts and issues arise as a result of the financial details. These must be considered accordingly.

The financial position will include details of income, assets, living expenditure and debts. The format of this information will vary among different agencies but details will usually include:

- income from all sources such as wages, pension, board, maintenance, family allowance and overtime;
- taxation deductions, which must be checked for accuracy;
- assets—the type and their market value;
- living expenditure such as food, clothing, transport, education;
- debts:
    - the name of the credit provider
    - the type of debt
    - account number
    - monthly repayment
    - total owing
    - whether secured or unsecured
    - any guarantor
    - arrears
    - interest rate charged
    - notices received
    - arrangements made
    - name, address and telephone number of any contact person
    - legal action taken

When all the pieces of information are gathered, the counsellor puts them together to form a picture of the financial situation. The income and expenditure details will show the extent of the client's overcommitment and it is then that financial alternatives can be considered.

In broad terms, there are three alternatives available to people in financial difficulties. These are to adjust debt repayments, decrease expenditure and/or increase income. The many forms of assistance within these three main categories will be explored in Chapter 6.

If there are pressing problems, such as an impending court action or eviction, the client will need to be encouraged to make immediate decisions. The client will usually need more time to consider alternatives which will have long-term effects on their lifestyle, such as the selling of assets.

The counsellor must be careful not to place their own values and standards on the client by telling them what they 'should' or 'should not' do. Once the alternatives and the consequences of any decisions have been explored, the actual decisions made must be those of the client, not the counsellor.

Negligence

A financial counsellor can be made liable for giving inaccurate information which results in any loss to the client. It is therefore imperative to be protected by professional indemnity insurance.

You must be absolutely sure of your information, because if you give the impression that you have certain specialised knowledge, the client is legally entitled to rely on your advice. For instance, advice cannot be given based on the information in this book, which is too general to apply in a specific case. Particularly if legal advice is required, an expert must be consulted.

It can happen that the information provided by the counsellor is misinterpreted by the client. To help overcome such problems it is advantageous to provide a written statement of the decisions made in the interview, signed by the client and counsellor.

Final checklist

On completion of the interview the following will be required:

- a written consent by the client, if the counsellor is to negotiate on the client's behalf;
- a photocopy of the important documents—be sure to return the originals;
- a statement of the client's understanding of the terms of any oral contract;

- a referral for on-going counselling, if appropriate;

- an appointment, if a further interview is needed;

- a report of the interview, to be written as soon as possible; and

- follow-up work, which will include writing letters and obtaining feedback from clients, creditors and referral agencies.

Negotiation with credit providers

Ideally it is preferable for clients to be able to negotiate on their own behalf. Part of the educational and growth process in a financial counselling interview can be the learning of these skills. In order to negotiate, clients must understand their rights and obligations under their credit contracts, have a clear understanding of the offer to be made to each creditor and be aware of the consequences of any choices made regarding their commitments.

Negotiations can take place in writing, in person or over the telephone. The counsellor can assist the client by helping to write the necessary letters, attending an interview with the client or being on hand while the telephone call is made. Role playing the situation is also effective. In this way the client is taking control of his or her own situation and is learning from the experience.

Nevertheless in most cases it will be necessary for the counsellor to negotiate on the client's behalf, at least for some of the debts. By the time many clients seek help from a financial counsellor, previous inappropriate arrangements have been made and broken. Most people are their own worst negotiators because of the lack of objectivity they have about their own situation. Add to this a communication barrier which can readily arise when promises are made and not kept, and you have the ingredients for an unsuccessful negotiation.

It may also be more appropriate for the counsellor to act on the client's behalf in situations where there are language difficulties, hearing disabilities or other problems which place the client in an inequitable position.

In a financial counselling agency, negotiations usually take place over the telephone. These may be initial negotiations which the credit provider requires in writing before approval, or final negotiations which the counsellor must confirm in writing.

Whether the negotiation takes place over the telephone or in writing, the credibility of the client, counsellor and agency is always at stake. Professionalism and accuracy are therefore paramount. Before any negotiations, the facts and figures must be checked and rechecked. Details of income, debts and amounts outstanding must be verified. And the offer to be made to the credit provider must be realistic.

A successful negotiation arises when each party benefits from the transaction. It is to the creditor's advantage to accept a viable arrangement because it is always better to have a small regular repayment than no payment at all. Even when the negotiation is for the postponement of repayments or for the debt to be written off, once the credit provider has the facts to hand an informed decision can be made. This will mean a subsequent saving of time and administrative costs to the credit provider, and the client will also benefit by being released from pressures to pay what cannot be afforded.

The arrangement to be offered to the credit provider will be based on the facts of the situation, a realistic appraisal of the financial position and the decisions made by the client. Important considerations will include the current and future needs of the client, the amount available to repay the debts after necessary living expenditure has been taken into account, and whether the problem is likely to be short- or long-term.

When negotiating, you are not usually dealing with someone who has social welfare training. The credit provider is not interested in an analysis of the social, emotional and psychological aspects of the client's financial problems. The person on the other end of the telephone just wants to do their job and that is to collect arrears of payments.

It will increase the counsellor's effectiveness to try to understand the position of the collections officer, who can be under substantial pressure to get names removed from an arrears list. Increasing this pressure by aggressively demanding that action be take by the collections officer to make right perceived social injustices will only produce a defensive and hostile reaction. Use your communication skills to gain the person's co-operation and respect. You are, after all, a counsellor.

The counsellor will be negotiating with a businessperson and must use a businesslike approach. This means being armed with all the facts. Your credibility will be readily diminished if the credit provider advises you of a debt not disclosed by your client. Be prepared for such a situation because the arrangement you intended to propose will be no longer feasible if another debt is in fact owing. A further interview with your client will be necessary and your next attempt at negotiating will be more difficult.

Preparation for the negotiation will include obtaining information about the credit provider, for instance, finding out who has authority to approve the arrangement you are proposing, be it the collections officer, the manager or someone higher up in the hierarchy. This will save valuable time. Also try to find out the name of the person to whom you will be speaking and have all the details to hand to readily identify the case. Most records are filed or placed on a computer under the person's account number and the counsellor should have this information readily available.

When making the telephone call ensure that you will not be interrupted. Be relaxed, assertive yet polite. Begin by establishing your credentials. Give your name, your function, the organisation you represent and say that you have the person's written authority to act on their behalf. When you provide the person's identifying details such as their name and account number, you will often find the collections officer will be well acquainted with the case. This means that there may be some preconceived ideas about your client and an initial response may be one of simmering anger with declarations of assistance previously provided and arrangements broken.

Exaggerations can take place on both sides and perceptions of the actual situation will depend on the particular person's point of view, be it the client or collections officer. The counsellor must attain an objective assessment by listening to what the person has to say and obtaining as much information as possible. Be aware of the limitations of the telephone. Without the aid of body language and the many other advantages of a face-to-face interview, voice tones and content can be easily misinterpreted.

When offering an arrangement, briefly outline the client's problem, present financial details and say what the client can afford to repay. Have the facts and figures readily available to answer any questions.

Let the credit provider know if other lenders have agreed to help. If others have seen benefit in helping your client, then this will make the creditor more receptive to your offer. If you are still unsuccessful with the collections officer or manager, tell them of the other options available to your client, such as talking to the general manager or taking the case to the Commercial Tribunal. Point to relevant legislation or the outcome of a particular court case that supports your client's right to the assistance. Above all be persistent.

After your successful negotiation, ensure that it is accurately recorded in your files and confirmation letters sent to the creditor and your client.

Letter-writing

Letters written by financial counsellors must be like their negotiations, businesslike and to the point. The rules of writing any business letter will apply. Find out the name of the person to whom you are writing: do not send a letter simply to a position, for example, the manager. Give an accurate reference, including the account number and the client's name and address. Only give as much information as is necessary, as clearly and accurately as possible. Care must be taken not to breach confidentiality. Forward a copy of the letter to your client or at least ensure they are aware of its contents.

Typical letters written by a financial counsellor include:

- a negotiation on the client's behalf;
- confirmation of a successful negotiation;

- a request for information such as a copy of a contract, detailed statement of account;

- an advice that your agency is no longer acting on the client's behalf, for example, if arrangements have not been maintained and attempts to contact the client have been unsuccessful;

- a standard letter for use by the client in negotiating their own arrangement. An example is given on page 63.

Report-writing

Throughout this chapter, the need for accuracy and detailed information has been stressed. This is equally important in the financial counsellor's report written after each interview.

The report will be an essential resource for negotiation, follow-up and future action. It must be factual and readily comprehensible, as it may need to be used by someone other than the interviewer, for instance, if another counsellor has to take over the case.

The confidentiality of the client must be protected and the file should be made accessible to the client if required. Judgmental opinions and criticisms have no place on such a file. Extreme care must be taken in writing a report, which can be subpoenaed for a court hearing.

The format of a report will largely be determined by the policy of a particular agency. Nevertheless it is helpful in a financial counselling report to follow a plan. Information can be grouped under appropriate headings such as social and family factors, emotional and health factors, financial position, decisions made by the client, alternatives considered and follow-up work.

Although much of the financial information will already be included in the income/expenditure sheets, other details, such as arrangements with creditors and legal action taken, will need to be noted. A report of the alternatives considered at the interview will help in reviewing a case and ensuring that all relevant in-

---

Address
Date

Mr/Mrs/Miss/Ms ....
Title ....
Company ....
Address ....

Dear Mr/Mrs/Miss/Ms ....

Account Number ....

I am writing to request a variation of my contract with you.

For the past ...... (weeks, months) I have been ...... (unemployed, on workers' compensation, etc.) and it will be ...... (weeks, months) before I can resume normal repayments.

In order to improve my situation, I am receiving financial counselling and approaching my creditors for assistance. The ...... (Building Society, Department Store, Credit Union, etc.) has agreed to ...... (postpone repayment, reduce repayments, etc.).

I have enclosed a statement of my income and expenditure and request your assistance by ...... (freezing the interest on my account, deferring repayments for ......, accepting monthly repayments of $...... for ...... months, etc.).

Your early reply would be appreciated.

Yours faithfully

Name ....

---

formation has been covered. It will also provide protection to the counsellor, if the information given at the interview is refuted by the client.

The main disadvantage of a file is that a person's situation changes and the information contained on a file can lead to prejudging of a subsequent interview. People and their circumstances change, and it must be recognised that it is what a person is saying here and now that is relevant. Therefore the counsellor should consider the point at which a file no longer serves any purpose.

6

Alternatives for the client

In financial counselling there are three main financial alternatives that can be considered by clients. These are:

1. adjusting debt repayments;
2. decreasing expenditure; and/or
3. increasing income.

These alternatives will be considered in greater detail in this chapter.

1. Adjusting debt repayments

Before considering the adjusting of debt repayments, it is essential to ensure that the debt is in fact owed and the amount being claimed is correct. All documentation must be thoroughly checked, to see whether contracts and procedures have complied with relevant legislation and to make sure that interest and other charges have been accurately calculated.

If the debt is owed there are several types of arrangements that may be negotiated with the credit provider. The type of arrangement offered to the creditor will depend on the income available to the client after the necessary living expenses have been deducted. In most cases a credit provider will accept a viable arrangement, which is preferable to receiving no payment at all or pursuing legal action.

Arrangements can include a deferment of repayments, a reduction in repayments, pro-rating, capitalisation of arrears, debt consolidation, term extension and writing off the debt.

(a) Deferring repayments

A deferment, or postponement, of repayments means that the debtor is not required by the creditor to make a certain number of repayments. It is important in this situation to try and have the interest charges frozen or the debt will increase while repayments are not being made. This type of arrangement is helpful when a short-term crisis such as temporary illness has affected the client's income and a return to an income level enabling maintenance of normal repayments is expected.

(b) Reducing repayments

A reduction in repayments means that the creditor agrees to accept a lesser repayment for a certain period or until the debt is finalised. Again it is important to have the interest charges frozen or the debt will continue to increase while the reduced repayments are being maintained. Such an arrangement can help when there is a limited surplus available to repay debts after the deduction of necessary living expenses.

(c) Pro-rating

Pro-rating occurs when a limited amount is available to repay several creditors. Each creditor in this instance would receive a fair share percentage of the sum available. This may be calculated in several ways, for instance a percentage of the monthly repayments or of the balance of the loans. Consider the situation of Mr Trill. After developing a viable money plan, Mr Trill finds that he has $300 per month available to repay his creditors. Mr Trill has the following debts:

Creditor	Monthly Repayment ($)
ABC Finance Company	200
XYZ Bank	100
LMN Visa Card	60
HIJ Department Store	40

As the $300 available to Mr Trill equals 75 per cent of the $400 to be paid monthly to the creditors, a possible arrangement would be:

Creditor	Calculation ($)	Monthly Repayment ($)
ABC Finance Company	200 × 75%	150
XYZ Bank	100 × 75%	75
LMN Visa Card	60 × 75%	45
HIJ Department Store	40 × 75%	30

An alternative calculation is the unit method. For example, Mr Grant has $440 per month available to repay debts totalling $10,000. The debts are as follows:

Creditor	Balance ($)	No. of Units
ABC Finance Company	7000	7 units
XYZ Bank	2000	2 units
LMN Visa Card	1000	1 unit
HIJ Department Store	1000	1 unit
		11 units

As there is $440 per month available, this can be divided by 11 to give the dollar value of each unit. In this case each unit would be worth $40. Therefore a possible arrangement would be:

Creditor	Calculation ($)	Monthly Repayment ($)
ABC Finance Company	40 × 7 units	280
XYZ Bank	40 × 2 units	80
LMN Visa Card	40 × 1 unit	40
HIJ Department Store	40 × 1 unit	40
		440

The unit method based on the outstanding balances of the debt is the calculation most commonly used by financial counsellors.

(d) Capitalisation

Capitalisation of arrears is the inclusion of outstanding repayments in the loan balance enabling the resumption of normal repayments. A capitalisation will mean that the term of the loan is extended, or the loan is recalculated to increase the repayment slightly and ensure that the loan is repaid within the original term.

This type of arrangement is of great benefit when adjusting large, long-term loans. For example, a client has been unemployed for several months and has fallen $2000 behind with repayments on a home loan. When resuming employment the person may find that they are able to pay an extra $50 per month towards the loan but this would not be a viable arrangement. Not only would it take many months to clear the arrears but extra interest would normally be charged until the outstanding repayments had been paid. A capitalisation would mean the immediate clearance of arrears avoiding any extra interest charges as well as the alleviation of financial pressures.

(e) Extending the term

A term extension enables the reduction of repayments by increasing the period of the loan. It is important to note that such a debt adjustment will mean an increase in the total amount to be re-paid, as interest will be charged for a longer period. Also a term extension will often only lower repayments by a few dollars and this must be considered against the increased cost involved. Nevertheless this form of arrangement may be a workable alternative to help balance a money plan.

(f) Consolidating debts

A debt consolidation is the combining of several high-interest-rate loans into one low-interest-rate loan. This can substantially reduce a borrower's outgoings: for example, in one case it was possible to reduce expenditure by more than $2000 per month. For such a consolidation, the borrower would have to meet normal lending guidelines and be able to afford the new loan. Particularly helpful in this area are work credit unions, which normally go to great lengths to assist their members.

The overall cost of a debt consolidation must be considered and consolidation through high-interest-rate finance avoided. Renegotiation of loans is sometimes offered as a 'way out' by lenders who offer to 'assist' by consolidating debts at very high rates of interest over a longer period. The total cost of such a loan can be exorbitant.

As a general rule, consider a bank or credit union consolidation. Most finance companies specialise in consolidation and charge a much higher rate of interest.

(g) Writing off a debt

A lender may agree to write off a debt, particularly if a small amount is owing and there is no possible way that the borrower can repay the loan even if legal action is taken. It may not be economically feasible for a lender to pursue such a debt, which may be claimed as a 'bad debt' against their taxation assessment. But because a 'write-off' may be recoverable at some future time, it is advisable to obtain a written confirmation from the creditor agreeing to forgo any future right of action.

Writing off a debt can greatly help a client on a very low income such as a pension or benefit, and may also be appropriate in other situations, such as cases of genuine hardship.

(h)   The Credit Acts

The recent Credit Acts have made certain arrangements with providers of regulated credit a requirement of law. For example, under the NSW Credit Act, if a borrower is having financial difficulties as a result of hardship an approach can be made to the lender to reduce and/or postpone repayments. To get this assistance, the debtors must reasonably expect that it would enable them to discharge their obligations.

If the lender will not agree to the arrangement, the borrower can approach the Commissioner of Consumer Affairs for a variation. If the Commissioner agrees that the borrower has a valid case, then negotiations can be made to vary the contract. If this is unsuccessful, the matter will be referred to the Commercial Tribunal, which can make binding orders to assist the borrower. These orders can include a variation in repayments or in the terms of a contract or even the postponement of repossession of goods.

Similarly, under the Credit (Home Finance Contracts) Act, 1984 (NSW), a debtor experiencing hardship can seek relief in relation to a home mortgage contract of less than $67,500.

The debtor can approach the credit provider to extend the term of the contract and/or postpone repayments if there are reasonable expectations that this assistance will enable repayments to be maintained.

If the creditor refuses to help, the matter can be considered by the Commissioner of Consumer Affairs and will then be referred to the Commercial Tribunal if negotiations between the Commissioner and creditor are unsuccessful. The Tribunal can order a variation of the contract and postpone repayments for as long as six months.

(i)   Government assistance

Certain forms of government assistance can also aid in the adjustment of debt repayments. Examples of such assistance would include the mortgage relief schemes and provision of Co-operative Housing Society Loans. These have restrictive guidelines which vary between the states, and are subject to regular changes.

The NSW Mortgage Relief Scheme is funded by the State and Federal Governments and provides short-term financial assistance to people who are experiencing difficulties in repaying their home loans as a result of unforeseen changes in circumstances. The Scheme is administered by the Department of Housing and is available to borrowers with a gross family income of less than $27,600, where the balance of the mortgages amounts to less than $67,500. Assistance is by an interest-free loan to a maximum of $5000. The money is paid directly to the lender to clear arrears and/or subsidise repayments. The borrower is expected to maintain repayments of 25 per cent of their gross income towards their home loan and to come to an arrangement to repay the mortgage relief as soon as possible.

In cases of extreme hardship, the NSW Co-operative Housing Societies will provide low-interest finance to low-income earners in order to discharge an existing home mortgage. Initially permission must be sought from the Co-operative Housing Societies' Special Eligibility Committee, and stringent guidelines on income, the amount to be borrowed and the value of the house must be met. If successful, the person's name is placed on a loan request list, in sequence of application and degree of need. The main problem with such a scheme is the waiting time before a loan becomes available. Therefore sufficient interim measures must be taken to prevent the existing mortgage from increasing or repossession taking place.

(j) Legal action

If arrangements cannot be successfully negotiated with a credit provider and legal action ensues, immediate steps must be taken to prevent a judgment being entered. The remedies available to debtors and creditors are discussed in Chapter 7. For ordinary unsecured debts of less than $5000, which are recovered through the local courts in New South Wales, it is never too late to enter an out-of-court arrangement with the lender. As long as no further legal action is taken, this will save legal costs and the many other pressures associated with court actions.

Bankruptcy can be an option of last resort in adjusting debt repayments. It is a remedy available to both the credit provider and the debtor. A person can apply to become voluntarily bankrupt, or a creditor can apply to the court for an order declaring the debtor bankrupt if the debt is greater that $1500. Voluntary bankruptcy can benefit a person whose only source of income is a pension, who has no assets and no likelihood of being able to repay their debts. In such cases a person will generally be released from bankruptcy after three years. Bankruptcy is discussed in greater detail in Chapter 7.

2. Decreasing expenditure

Expenses are decreased by the adjustment of debt repayments; but it may be the case that the client is experiencing financial difficulties even though they have no credit commitments; the client may need debt adjustment as well as other assistance to balance the budget.

(a) Expenditure alternatives

Before any alternative is considered, there must be an appreciation of the client's values, standards and goals. A money plan can then be developed and priorities assessed. Then expenditure may be able to be decreased on certain luxury items.

In some cases it is possible to reduce spending on necessities such as food by improving shopping and cooking skills and knowledge of nutrition. Inexpensive leisure alternatives may also be appropriate, for example, stress management and relaxation classes may be an alternative to sedatives, quit-smoking programs may be an alternative to an expensive smoking habit. Or establishing a goal to save for a special regular outing may help limit the amount spent weekly at the pub. There are also free or inexpensive holiday homes and vacation camps available through various government and church organisations for children and families.

(b) Credit cards

A reassessment of priorities may lead to the client deciding no longer to use their credit cards. The cards can be returned to the credit provider and an arrangement could possibly be made to freeze the interest and repay the balance outstanding in affordable instalments. This can lead to reduced expenditure and an improvement in future spending patterns. Alternatives to buying on credit, such as lay-bys and saving for desired goods, can help overcome the temptation to buy and the instant gratification of having the goods straight away that results from using a credit card.

(c) Selling assets

A realistic appraisal of a person's financial position may mean that difficult decisions will have to be made. A credit provider will probably be unwilling to help a borrower until they have taken all possible steps to improve their own situation. This may mean the necessary sale of assets, such as the sale of a car to pay out a hire-purchase loan or the sale of a block of land to discharge several high-interest loans that can no longer be maintained. The sale of assets may be the only means a person has of being able to keep the possessions that are most valued, as well as maintain necessary living expenditure. It is important to remember that it is what the client values that matters; it is not a decision to be made by the counsellor, who will usually have different priorities.

(d) Concessions and rebates

For people trying to survive on a pension or benefit it is essential to be aware of the concessions and rebates available to them, which can substantially reduce living expenditure. These can include reductions on telephone rentals and electricity accounts, rebates on council and water rates, free driver's licences, assistance with furniture removal, discounts on Commonwealth Government publications and on admissions to some theatres and sporting events, and some sales tax exemptions.

(e) Material aid

Low-income earners may also need to obtain emergency assistance from material-aid sources such as the Smith Family, St Vincent de Paul or the Red Cross. This may take the form of basic necessities such as food and clothing or help with urgent bills like gas and electricity. Access to this type of assistance may be vital in making ends meet.

3. Increasing income

This may prove to be the most difficult alternative to carry out, with high unemployment and stringent limits on the earning capacity of social security recipients. Nevertheless people can be truly ingenious in finding ways to increase their income, once they can see their financial situation realistically.

(a) Employment

The obvious way to increase income is to obtain employment. What is not always apparent is the variety of ways in which income can be produced. Often people have skills, hobbies or even original ideas which can provide a necessary extra source of income.

Such small starts have in some cases led to successful businesses. One woman who started to make pies at home to supplement a pension began by selling to local shops and ended up with a thriving catering business. Resources such as the NSW Small Business Office can often help by giving expert advice and financial assistance for the establishment of viable small businesses. There are also many parents, who by choice or necessity stay at home to be with their children, who have supplemented their incomes by joining family day-care schemes and undertaking extra child-minding. Clients have found countless avenues for increasing their incomes.

(b) *Developing new skills*

When a person has suffered an illness or injury which precludes them from a former occupation, it can be helpful to become involved in a rehabilitation or retraining program or to do some voluntary work. For people wishing to develop new skills and improve employment prospects, there are also numerous courses available through colleges of technical and further education. Many courses are specifically designed to assist migrants and youth, groups which have particular difficulties in securing employment in our society.

(c) *Income supplements*

It is essential for a counsellor to check that a person in receipt of a pension or benefit is receiving their correct social security entitlements, and that families on very low incomes are aware of income supplements, as well as education bursaries and allowances available from State and Federal Governments.

(d) *Family maintenance*

In some cases supporting parents have not pursued their right to maintenance, which could substantially alleviate income deficiencies. The reasons for this are many and can include simply not knowing how to go about obtaining maintenance or not wanting to pursue the other party for emotional reasons. Correct information and appropriate counselling to work through these feelings can be of great help here. There are many excellent marital counselling services throughout Australia to which appropriate referrals can be made. For example, the Family Court Counselling Service, as well as providing individual counselling for people who have separated, conducts public information sessions. The Family Court also produces films and pamphlets, which include:

Counselling at the Family Court—Things You May Like to Know

Thinking About Separating?

Family Law and You

Family Law—Lawyers, Legal Costs, Legal Aid

Marital Separation—How it Affects Children

The Importance of Access For You and Your Children

Property Settlements in the Family Court

A booklet titled *Parenting After Separation: Practical Information and Guidelines* has been prepared by the Family Court of Australia Court Counselling Service, Sydney Registry.

It is important to consider the impact on social security entitlements which the receipt of maintenance will have, although in certain limited circumstances maintenance payments are not treated as income.

(e) Sharing accommodation

There are other practical and simple ways of increasing income which may require the working through of emotional blocks or just accurate information before the alternatives become acceptable to the client and therefore viable. These can range from sharing accommodation to completing an income tax return.

Sharing accommodation can be an obvious way of making ends meet which is rarely thought of in our society of insular, nuclear families living in their separate modes of accommodation. Of course there are always problems to overcome when another person enters a household but these difficulties are usually surmountable and are often preferable to having to lose the home altogether because it can no longer be afforded.

Naturally *extreme* care must be taken when choosing someone to share a home. In the case of a widow who is left in a large house by herself because the family has grown up and moved away, the financial strain of maintaining a home can be unmanageable, but having to sell the house and move away from a familiar environment, which provides supportive social networks, can also have disastrous effects. A suitable boarder can provide the necessary extra income to pay the household bills such as council and water rates and enable essential house repairs.

If the house is mortgaged, it is necessary to check the lender's policy on sharing the house. In some instances, this will change the occupational status of the dwelling, resulting in an increase in the interest charged on the mortgage.

Again it is important to consider the effect a boarder may have on social security entitlements. In certain cases the possibility of Housing Commission accommodation should be explored.

(f) Taxation

It can often be the case that clients who have not completed income tax returns simply do not realise that they actually have money owing to them from the Taxation Department. A refund in this situation can make all the difference in balancing a budget.

For those who may not be able to afford professional help from an accountant or tax agent there are other sources of information and help, for example, in July and August each year some accountants donate their time to assist people through many Community Advice Bureaus. Also in cases of serious financial hardship, an application can be made under section 265 of the Income Tax Assessment Act 1936, to be released from paying a taxation debt. A valuable guide for counsellors can be found in the *Tax Kit* prepared by the Financial Counsellors' Association of Australia.

7

Debt and legal action

In the states of Australia where the new credit legislation has
been implemented, there is now additional relief available to
debtors as an alternative to the action being taken through the
court system. Nevertheless where the protection provided by
the Credit Acts is not sought by the debtor and where debts
are not regulated by this legislation, creditors can continue to
recover debts through the courts. Such a dual system exists in
New South Wales which will be the example discussed in this
chapter.

Debt recovery and the Credit Act, 1984

The NSW Credit Act ('the Act') gives certain rights to borrowers
of regulated credit who are in financial difficulties. Generally,
credit is regulated by the Act where the contract was entered into
after 28 February 1985, the amount involved does not exceed
$20,000 and the interest rate is greater than 14 per cent. This
would include credit obtained from finance companies as well as
continuing credit contracts such as Bankcards.

If a borrower falls behind in repaying any regulated credit
commitments, then in most cases the creditor must serve a section 107 notice on the debtor and any guarantor before starting
any legal action. If the debt is a continuing credit contract, a
statement of account and a request for payment must also be
enclosed.

The section 107 notice must specify:

- the default of the debtor;

- that the credit provider intends to exercise rights and remedies unless within one month the default is remedied and the amounts due are paid;

- whether the amounts due under the contract increase until paid.

The credit provider is required to include with the notice a prescribed form, Credit Regulation, clause 16, as follows:

Form 7.

(Cl. 16.)

WHAT SHOULD I DO NOW THAT I HAVE RECEIVED THIS NOTICE?

1. You should discuss this matter with your credit provider or mortgagee as soon as possible. You may be able to work out some other arrangement about your contract. For example, you could ask for your contract to be varied, repayments to be deferred, or action postponed.

   The person to contact is ....
   (name or title of officer/s)

   of ....
   (name of credit provider or mortgagee)

   ....
   (address)
   ....

   Telephone No./s: ....

2. If you cannot come to a suitable arrangement with your credit provider or mortgagee, contact Consumer Affairs immediately. If you have been **unemployed, sick** or there is another **good reason** why you are having problems with your contract, then your contract may be able to be varied under the law to meet your situation.

   There are other people, such as financial counsellors, who may be able to help.

3. If you disagree with anything in this notice, including what it says you owe, contact Consumer Affairs or get legal advice immediately.

The creditor is not required to serve the notice and prescribed form if:

- there are reasonable grounds to believe that he was induced to enter the contract or mortgage by fraudulent misrepresentation on the part of the debtor or that mortgaged goods will be hidden, damaged or disposed of; or

- after making reasonable efforts, the debtor or mortgagor cannot be located.

After receiving the section 107 notice, the debtor has one month to come to an arrangement with the credit provider. If the debtor has fallen behind with repayments as a result of hardship such as illness or unemployment then the Act provides certain rights. Under the Act, the debtor suffering hardship can seek a postponement of repayment and/or term extension. To obtain this assistance, debtors must reasonably expect that this measure would enable them to discharge their obligations.

If an arrangement cannot be negotiated then the Commissioner for Consumer Affairs can be asked to mediate. If the Commissioner is unable to reach a satisfactory solution, the matter can be referred to the Commercial Tribunal. Such an application prevents any further action being taken by the creditor to enforce the debt until a decision has been reached by the Tribunal.

The Commercial Tribunal consists of a Chairman sitting alone or with representatives from industry and consumer interests. At the hearing a debtor can put their own case to the Tribunal or obtain legal representation. The Tribunal has wide powers to assist debtors in financial difficulties. Assistance can include an order to vary the contract, for example, by postponing or reducing repayments. Orders made by the Tribunal are binding on debtors and creditors and can be enforced by any court of competent jurisdiction.

Where a goods mortgage has been given as security for the provision of regulated credit, the Act provides certain protection to the mortgagor. If the mortgagor falls behind with repayments, the credit provider must give one month's notice of intention to repossess the mortgaged goods. During this period the mortgagor can come to an arrangement with the creditor to vary the contract or postpone action. If this is unsuccessful the mortgagor can seek assistance from the Department of Consumer Affairs.

Under the Act no one can enter a person's home to repossess goods without the owner's permission or a court order. Further, if three-quarters of the amount of finance has been repaid, the goods cannot be repossessed without an order from the Tribunal. If the matter is referred to the Commercial Tribunal, orders can be made to stop the repossession or to prevent repossessed goods being sold.

Debt recovery and the local court

Where the Credit Act does not apply or where a debtor has not sought to pursue his or her rights under the Act, the lender can enforce the debt through the courts. In New South Wales the local court hears claims up to a limit of $5000, the District Court hears claims up to $100,000 and the Supreme Court hears matters to any amount.

As financial counsellors are most often called on to help borrowers who have small, unsecured debts, the system of debt recovery in the local courts in New South Wales will be considered in this section. These unsecured debts can include credit cards, department store accounts and credit obtained from banks, building societies, credit unions and finance companies.

Before starting legal action, a creditor or debt collection agency will send one or more letters of demand to the debtor. These letters will usually state the amount of arrears and advise that unless these are cleared by a certain date, legal action will begin.

It is imperative at this stage that a detailed statement of account is obtained from the creditor and that calculations and contracts are checked to ensure that the debt is owed and the amount claimed is correct. A financial counselling interview can then help a debtor to determine the best course of action, for example, by negotiating an arrangement or making an application to the Consumer Claims Tribunal.

A money plan may show that after necessary living expenses have been deducted there is enough income available to offer an arrangement to the lender. Any arrangement must be confirmed in writing and a copy of the letter kept. If subsequent legal action is taken, and it can be shown that an arrangement was made and maintained, then the debtor may not be required to pay legal costs.

The Consumer Claims Tribunal can assist debtors where the amount involved is less than $3000, the contract is less than two years old and where no proceedings have already begun in another court or tribunal. The Consumer Claims Tribunal is of particular assistance where the debt is in relation to defective goods or services. The parties are not represented by lawyers and costs are not awarded. The Tribunal has the power to grant relief from payment of a debt based on 'fairness and equitableness'.

Starting legal action

If a satisfactory arrangement cannot be negotiated or the debtor ignores the letter of demand, the creditor can then start legal action.

The first step in the court process is the issuing of a summons, usually a Plaint and Default Summons from the local court (see page 83). The summons is normally served on the debtor by a process server or the court bailiff. A summons can be legally served in a number of ways; for example, it may be served on anyone in the debtor's home who is apparently over the age of 16 years.

If the debtor has not received the summons and further action has been taken, legal advice should be sought, as it may be possible to have the judgment set aside. If the debtor is actually avoiding service of the summons or for some other reason the summons cannot be served, the creditor can apply for an order for 'substituted service'. In this way the summons may be posted to the debtor's last known place of residence.

When a summons has been served

A debtor must act quickly on receiving a summons because the creditor can obtain a judgment 14 days after service.

There are several options available to the debtor which include paying the total amount due, entering into an informal agreement with the creditor, or filing one of the following:

Form 12

Local Courts (Civil Claims) Act, 1970
Sections 22 and 24

PLAINT AND DEFAULT SUMMONS COMMENCING ACTION

Issued from the Local Court
at
in the State of New South Wales.

Plaint No.:

Plaintiff:

of:

Name of solicitor
or agent acting:

of:

Ref:

Defendant:

of:

Particulars of Claim:

Amount claimed	$	Additional service fees $
Issue and service fee	$	
Professional costs	$	
Total claimed	$	

It is claimed on the basis of the particulars stated (or attached) that you owe the plaintiff the amount shown above. Unless you take action in accordance with the provisions of the abovementioned Act, Judgment may be entered up against you for the amount claimed and costs without further notice to you.

Dated:

Registrar

Information to help you

1. There are certain courses of action available to you in this matter, which are too numerous to be fully explained in this Summons.

2. If you do not do anything **within 14 days** of receiving this Summons, your legal rights may be adversely affected. Also you may have to pay extra costs.

3. If you do not understand what this Summons means, or what you should do, then **you should seek legal advice.** If you do not have a solicitor, then the staff at any Local Court will help you **free of charge.** Advice specifically related to your circumstances may then be given.

4. If you telephone, call personally, or write to the court about this Summons, you must refer to the **plaint number,** which is shown at the top of this Summons. Telephone No:

AFFIDAVIT OF SERVICE (For office use only)	DEFAULT SUMMONS

AFFIDAVIT OF SERVICE
(For office use only)

I, ...
of ....
....
make oath and say: ....
I am ....
....
I did on the ....day of ....
19 , duly serve

in this action with a copy of the within summons by
delivering it to ....
....
....
at ....
....
....
....

SWORN at

this   day of
              19   , ...

before me,

A Justice of the Peace

DEFAULT SUMMONS

In the Local Court
at
in the State of New South Wales.

Plaint No.   19

PLAINTIFF:

DEFENDANT:

MINUTE OF JUDGMENT
(For office use only)

Judgment by

Plaintiff for:

	$	c
Claim:		
Costs:		
Professional costs:		
TOTAL		

Date:

Registrar

- an Agreement as to Claim;

- a Statement of Confession of Claim;

- a Notice of Grounds of Defence; and/or

- a Notice of Set-Off.

If there are grounds for defending the action or the debtor has a claim against the creditor, legal advice should be sought. Free legal advice can be obtained from legal centres or from the Chamber Magistrate at the local court.

In a Statement of Confession of Claim (see page 87), the debtor can admit to the whole or part of the amount owing. Filing the 'Confession' for the amount claimed on the summons means that judgment by Confession is entered for that amount, and the debt becomes legally enforceable. If the debt is owed, this action will help the debtor by avoiding the extra legal costs involved in the creditor obtaining a default judgment and by freezing the interest charged on the debt at 18.25 per cent, or the current rate of court interest.

At the time of filing the Confession it is essential to also complete an Application to Pay by Instalments (see page 87) and an Affidavit as to Property and Means, otherwise the whole of the debt confessed to will become payable. The instalment application sets down the terms of repayment offered by the debtor.

Once this application is accepted by the Registrar, the credit provider has 14 days in which to object. If no objection is lodged with the court, then the terms of the instalment order become binding on the debtor and the creditor. If an objection is lodged, the matter is decided before a magistrate. A debtor can apply to have an instalment order altered if there are changes in his or her circumstances. It is more difficult for a creditor to have an instalment order varied, and significant financial improvement in the debtor's situation would have to be shown.

An Application to Pay by Instalments can be an important option available to the debtor at any stage once legal action has begun. It is imperative that this application is based on a viable money plan. Although a successful instalment application prevents the creditor taking further recovery action at that point, if a debtor misses a payment then the creditor can recommence enforcement proceedings.

The judgment debt

If a debtor receives a summons and takes none of the abovementioned steps within 14 days of service, the credit provider can obtain a default judgment against the debtor. This is merely an administrative process which takes place when the creditor files an Affidavit of Service and an Affidavit of Debt at the court.

Once judgment is entered the debt becomes legally enforceable. The costs involved are added to the existing debt and the interest charged on the debt is frozen at 18.25 per cent.

At this stage, if the debtor has a case for setting the judgment aside, for example, if the debt is not owed, legal advice should be sought and the appropriate documents lodged with the court. These can include an Application to Set Aside Judgment or Order, a Notice of Defence and an Application for Stay of Proceedings.

If the debt is owed, the debtor can come to an arrangement with the creditor or can prevent further legal action being taken to enforce the debt by filing an Application to Pay by Instalments. If accepted by the Registrar and the creditor, this application becomes binding on the debtor and creditor.

Unfortunately all too often the debtor takes no action after receiving notice of the judgment. This enables the creditor to take further action to enforce the judgment debt. This action can include an Examination Summons, a Garnishee Order or a Writ of Execution.

Examination Summons

An Examination Summons is an order for the debtor to appear before the court to be examined about his or her financial situation. The summons will list the documents that the debtor must

LOCAL COURTS (CIVIL CLAIMS) ACT, 1970
Sections 28 (1) and 40 (2) (a)
(TO BE COMPLETED IN TRIPLICATE)

Statement of Confession of Claim and/or
Application to Pay by Instalments

In the Local Court
at
in the State of New South Wales.

Plaint No.:

Plaintiff:

Defendant:
Address for service
of notices is:

Statement of Confession*   Form 17

I, the defendant in this action, do hereby confess that the sum of
$ being (part of*) the amount claimed by the plaintiff, is due to the plaintiff
from the defendant in full satisfaction of the plaintiff's claim.**

Dated:

Defendant

Signed in the presence of:

Signature:

Full name:

Address:

#Qualification:

Application to Pay by Instalments*   Form 26

I hereby apply for an order that (the unpaid amount of the judgment debt)* (the amount to which I have
confessed)* herein be paid by instalments of

$
per

commencing on

Dated:

Defendant/Judgment Debtor*

NOTE: The Affidavit as to Property and Means overleaf must be completed where an application is made to pay by instalments.

* Delete if not applicable.

** Do not include any amount in respect of courts costs or professional costs.

The Statement of Confession has no force of effect for the purposes of section 28 of the abovementioned Act unless the signature of every person executing it, other than a barrister or attorney, is witnessed by a registrar, a clerk in the office of the registrar, a clerk of the Local Court, an attorney or a justice of the peace.

 M.N. 217 L.O. 1149   (SEE OVER)

AFFIDAVIT AS TO PROPERTY AND MEANS

I

of

make oath and say:

I am the within named judgment debtor.

The following is a statement of my present assets, income and liabilities:

INCOME

$	p.w.	Net (wage or equivalent)
$	p.w.	Social security
$	p.w.	Child endowment
$	p.w.	Income of husband/wife
$	p.w.	
$	p.w.	
$	p.w.	TOTAL

DEBTS AND LIABILITIES: (Credit cards/ personal loans)

		Owing to:	Balance:
$	p.w.		
$	p.w.		
$	p.w.		
$	p.w.	TOTAL	

REGULAR EXPENSES:

$	p.w.	Mortgage re-payments
$	p.w.	Rent or board
$	p.w.	Rates (council and water)
$	p.w.	Food
$	p.w.	Gas/electricity
$	p.w.	Telephone
$	p.w.	Fares
$	p.w.	Petrol
$	p.w.	School expenses
$	p.w.	Insurance/superannuation
$	p.w.	Hospital/medical fund
$	p.w.	
$	p.w.	
$	p.w.	
$	p.w.	
$	p.w.	TOTAL

HOUSE OR LAND:

Value of house/land $
Mortgage $

Location:

OTHER PROPERTY: (Not under hire purchase)

$	Motor vehicle No.:
$	Furniture
$	Electrical goods
$	Shares or investments

BANK AND BUILDING SOCIETY ACCOUNTS:

Balance:	Name and Branch:
$	
$	

I support myself and   dependents.

Sworn at

    on

before me:

Justice of the Peace

APPLICATION GRANTED/REFUSED

Registrar
(date)

bring to the hearing, for example, income verification, copies of accounts, bank passbooks and so on. A fine can be imposed if the debtor fails to provide these documents. And if a debtor fails to attend the hearing a Warrant for Apprehension can be issued for the debtor to be brought before the court.

The examination hearing assists in helping the Registrar determine whether an instalment order should be made. It also provides information for the credit provider to decide what action should be taken next.

Garnishee Orders

There are several types of Garnishee Orders, the most common being an order for the garnishment of wages. Other Garnishee Orders can include the garnishee of bank accounts or of friends or relatives, who may owe money to the debtor.

There are two types of orders for the garnishment of wages. These are a 'once only order' and a 'continuous order'. The 'once only order' is for the garnishment of one week's wages. The 'continuous order' is for the garnishment of four weeks' wages. After the four-week period, the creditor must apply to the court for a further garnishee order.

The garnishment of wages means that the debtor may only receive from their weekly wages the equivalent of the Sydney basic wage less $8. The current Sydney basic wage for a male is $103.00 and for a female $93.70.

Orders for the garnishment of wages can mean further hardship to the debtor. Financial difficulties can be exacerbated when not enough is left in a person's pay packet to cover living expenditure and any other financial commitments the person may have. There can also be a stigma attached to such an order, with not only the embarrassment of an employer knowing about the debtor's financial problems but the possibility of the loss of a job as a result.

In order to stop garnishment of wages, the debtor can negotiate with the creditor or complete an application to pay by instalments. The instalment application will convert the continuous garnishee order into an Instalment Garnishee Order, which will continue on the repayment terms stated in the instalment application until the debt is repaid.

Writ of Execution

A Writ of Execution is an order to a bailiff of the court to take and sell certain possessions of the debtor. The debtor's goods are then sold at auction to pay the judgment debt.

On receipt of the writ, the bailiff will go to the residence of the debtor to notify the debtor of the writ and allow some time for the debtor to rectify the situation before executing the writ. The debtor at this stage can contact the creditor and come to an arrangement or make an Application to Pay by Instalments through the local court. The instalment application will stop the writ as long as the debtor maintains repayments under the terms of the instalment order.

If the debtor does nothing to stop the writ it will be executed by the bailiff, although the debtor can refuse to allow the bailiff into his or her residence. Items that can be sold include the debtor's personal possessions such as the car, television and stereo. But there are also certain goods that cannot be taken, such as necessary furniture, wearing apparel, tools of trade to the value of $500 and goods that are jointly owned.

A Writ of Execution (see page 91) is a common form of debt enforcement, but is not always taken to the final stage. This can be because debtors are so intimidated by such procedures that they come to some arrangement with the creditor and also because the sale of second-hand goods brings limited proceeds, and debtors in these circumstances often have little of value to be sold. The follow-through of the Writ of Execution is advantageous to the creditor where the debtor owns any land because once the personal property is sold, an application can be made to the District Court to sell the debtor's land to satisfy the remainder of the judgment debt.

Form 55

**Local Courts (Civil Claims) Act, 1970
(Section 58 (1))**

Application to Issue Execution

In the Local Court

at

in the State of New South Wales.

Plaint No.

Judgment
Creditor:

Address:

Judgment
Debtor:

Address for Execution:

$	— Unpaid judgment debt
$	— Fee for execution
$	— Professional costs (if any)
$	TOTAL

Judgment in this matter was given or entered

up on:

Pursuant to section 58 (1) of the abovementioned Act, I hereby apply for the issue of a writ of execution in this action.

The unpaid amount of the judgment debt in this matter is as shown above.

Dated:

(Attorney for the) Judgment Creditor.

When your client is owed money

It may be the case that your client is having financial difficulties as a result of customers not paying for goods or services supplied by your client. In this situation it may be necessary for the client to take legal action through the court to obtain the money owed.

It is important to ensure that the debt is enforceable and adequate notice is given to the debtor before taking legal action. Pursuing a debt through the courts can be a costly process especially if your client is unsuccessful with the claim. Legal advice should be sought from a chamber magistrate, a legal centre or other legal service as it may not be worth while for the client to pursue the debt.

If it is considered the appropriate course of action, and the debt is less than $5000, then a default summons can be filed at the local court. If the debtor does nothing within 14 days of the date of service of the summons, then judgment can be entered and the debt enforced through the procedures previously discussed.

Bankruptcy

There are two ways of becoming a bankrupt. A debtor can voluntarily apply to become bankrupt or a creditor can petition the Federal Court for an order declaring the debtor bankrupt.

Because the Bankruptcy Act 1966 is a Commonwealth statute, the laws are applicable throughout Australia and are dealt with by the Federal Courts. There are certain bars to becoming bankrupt, for example, a debtor cannot be forced into bankruptcy for less than $1500 or for an unliquidated debt (a debt where the exact amount owing has not been determined). Nevertheless a person can enter voluntary bankruptcy for any amount or can be made bankrupt where the aggregate debts of the petitioning creditor(s) amount to $1500.

If a debtor has been served with a bankruptcy notice and wants to avoid becoming bankrupt, immediate action must be taken.

The debtor usually only has 14 days in which to act and legal advice must be sought for the appropriate action to be taken.

Voluntary bankruptcy, although a remedy of last resort, is practically a daily occurrence in Australia. One of the main problems with voluntary bankruptcy is that unless financial counselling is received, the debtor may not learn how to cope financially in the future. Often people will become bankrupt more than once or children of people who have been bankrupt may also become bankrupts as adults, as this is the way they learnt to deal with their debts.

Financial counselling can help in this area first by considering alternatives to bankruptcy. If no alternatives exist the debtor can be assisted by:

- being helped through the bankruptcy process;

- learning skills such as money planning;

- increasing knowledge about the sources and costs of credit and the rights of consumers;

- gaining an insight into the reasons for debt problems so they are less likely to recur.

Voluntary bankruptcy is viewed with fear and seen as a stigma by many. It is important for debtors in this situation to understand that to become bankrupt is not a criminal offence and does not automatically mean that the debtor will never be granted credit again.

Becoming bankrupt voluntarily is simply a matter of completing certain forms such as a Debtor's Petition and a verified Statement of Affairs (see the forms reproduced between pages 94 and 103). If these forms are completed correctly they will be accepted by the Registrar in Bankruptcy and the debtor then becomes bankrupt.

Once declared bankrupt, the debtor's property vests in the Official Receiver in Bankruptcy. The debtor's estate is then administered either by a registered trustee or, more usually, by the Official Trustee (of the Official Receiver's Office).

BANKRUPTCY ACT 1966

DEBTOR'S PETITION

BANKRUPTCY DISTRICT OF

No.   of 19 .

Re:..

(a) Insert full name and address of debtor.

I, (a) ....

who reside at ....

and whose occupation is ....

petition the Registrar in Bankruptcy for the abovementioned Bankruptcy District

for the purpose of becoming a bankrupt by force of Section 55 of the Bankruptcy

Act.

(b) Here set out name and address of business (if any) carried on, liabilities of which are set out in the debtor's statement of affairs.

2. (b)

(c) If Petition is by majority of partners under S.56 of the Bankruptcy Act, set out that fact and names and addresses and occupations of all other partners.

3. (c)

DATED this   day of   19 .

Signed by the Debtor in my presence

Signature of Witness: ....

Address: **Debtor**

Occupation:

Presented this   day of   19

Accepted this   day of   19

at   o'clock in the   noon.

Registrar.

(No. 378)

BANKRUPTCY ACT

———

Affidavit Verifying Statement of Affairs

BANKRUPTCY DISTRICT OF   } No.   of 19

Re:

Ex parte:

(a) Full name, address and occupation.

I, (a)

of

make oath and say that the Statement of Affairs annexed to this Affidavit and

consisting of sheets numbered I. to VII. (inclusive) contains to the best of my

knowledge and belief a true and complete statement of my affairs as at the

(b) If creditor's petition, insert date of sequestration order; if debtor's petition, date of this affidavit.

(b)   day of   19

SWORN by the deponent   }

the   day of   }

                19   , at   }

Before me: }

Justice of the Peace.

BANKRUPTCY ACT

STATEMENT OF AFFAIRS

BANKRUPTCY DISTRICT OF

No.   of 19

Re:

Ex parte:

PART I.

Summary

Item No.	Liabilities	Amount	Item No.	Assets	Estimated Value
		$			$
1	Amount owing to unsecured creditors according to Part II.		1	Property specified in Part V.	
2	Amount by which the secured debts due to creditors exceed the value of the securities according to Part III.		2	Amount by which the secured debts due to creditors are less than the value of the securities according to Part III.	
3	Amount by which the debts in respect of hire-purchase agreements exceed the value of the properties held under the agreements according to Part IV.		3	Book debts according to Part VI.	
4	Total Surplus (if any)		4	Amount by which the debts in respect of hire-purchase agreements are less than the value of the properties held under the agreements according to Part IV.	
			5	Total Deficiency (if any)	
	TOTAL			TOTAL	

BANKRUPTCY ACT

PART II.

Unsecured Creditors

(Names must be arranged in alphabetical order and numbered consecutively.)

Column 1 No.	Column 2 Name	Column 3 Address	Column 4 Amount of Debt	Column 5 Year when Contracted	Column 6 Nature of Debt
			$		

NOTES.—1. Where a creditor owes moneys to the debtor and the amount owing by the creditor is less than the amount owing to the creditor, particulars of these amounts are to be included in this Part and not in Part VI. Particulars of these amounts are to be set out in column 3 immediately below the address of the creditor, as follows:—

Amount owing to creditor $
Amount owing by creditor $

The balance only is to be set out in column 4.

2. If a creditor holds a bill of exchange or a promissory note, particulars of the bill of exchange or promissory note so held are to be set out in column 2 immediately below the name of the creditor.

BANKRUPTCY ACT

PART II.

Unsecured Creditors

(Names must be arranged in alphabetical order and numbered consecutively.)

Column 1 No.	Column 2 Name	Column 3 Address	Column 4 Amount of Debt	Column 5 Year when Contracted	Column 6 Nature of Debt
			$		

NOTES.—1. Where a creditor owes moneys to the debtor and the amount owing by the creditor is less than the amount owing to the creditor, particulars of these amounts are to be included in this Part and not in Part VI. Particulars of these amounts are to be set out in column 3 immediately below the address of the creditor, as follows:—

Amount owing to creditor —— $

Amount owing by creditor —— $

The balance only is to be set out in column 4.

2. If a creditor holds a bill of exchange or a promissory note, particulars of the bill of exchange or promissory note are held are to be set out in column 2 immediately below the name of the creditor.

BANKRUPTCY ACT

PART III.

Secured Creditors

No.	Name of Creditor	Address	Amount of Debt $	Year when Contracted	Particulars of Security	Date when given	Estimated value of security at present $	Estimated Deficiency $	Estimated Surplus $
		Total $				Total $			

BANKRUPTCY ACT
Part IV.
Hire Purchase Agreements

No.	Name of Finance Company	Address	Date of Agreement	Particulars of goods under Agreement	Arrears of hire (if any)	Amount required to complete Agreement	Present value of goods	Estimated Surplus	Estimated Deficiency
					$	$	$	$	$
			TOTAL						

Notes: 1. Credit sales or terms sales are not to be included in this Part, but to be included in Part II.
2. Where goods previously held under hire purchase agreement have been repossessed and sold, the balance owing (if any) is to be shown in Part II.

BANKRUPTCY ACT

PART V.

Property

NATURE OF PROPERTY	ESTIMATED VALUE
	$
1. Cash at Bank (Name of Bank)	
2. Cash in hand	
3. Cash deposited with Solicitor (if any) for costs of petition or other proceedings	
4. Stock in Trade (at cost $) situated at	
5. Machinery, situated at	
6. Trade fixtures, Fittings, Utensils, etc., situated at	
7. Farming Stock, situated at	
8. Growing Crops, situated at	
9. Household Furniture and Effects, situated at	
10. Stocks and Shares	
11. Interest under Will, Deed of Settlement, etc., as follows	
12. Real Property not shown in Part III.	
13. Leasehold Property, situated at	
14. Motor Vehicles (Make ; Model	
15. Securities held (for example: by way of Mortgage, Bill of Sale, etc.)	
16. Other Property, namely (specify particulars)	
TOTAL	

Note: This Part should contain full particulars of every description of property in which the Bankrupt has an interest, being property defined by subsection (1) of Section 5 of the Bankruptcy Act, 1966, except property of which particulars are set out in Part III or Part IV

BANKRUPTCY ACT

PART VI.

Debts Due to the Estate

Column 1 No.	Column 2 Name of Debtor	Column 3 Address	Column 4 Amount of Debt $	Column 5 Amount likely to be received $

Note: Where the Estate owes money to a debtor and the amount owing by the Estate is less than the amount owing to the Estate, particulars of these amounts are to be included in this Part and not in Part II.

Particulars of these amounts are to be set out in column 3 immediately under the address of the debtor, as follows:—
Amount owing to the Estate $
Amount owing by the Estate $
The balance only is to be set out in column 4.

BANKRUPTCY ACT

PART VII.

General

1. I am not an undischarged bankrupt or insolvent under a Commonwealth Act or under a State Act and I have never previously become a bankrupt (except on the

   day of   19   ).

2. I have not previously compounded with my creditors or made any assignment or arrangement for the benefit of my creditors (except on the   day of

   19   ).

3. I have not during the past 5 years carried on business on my own account or in partnership

   OR

3. I have during the past 5 years carried on business on

   my own account   as a   , and have kept the following books of
   in partnership

   account in connexion with that business:—

4. Particulars of my contingent liabilities and any other liabilities not specified in a previous Part of this Statement are:—

5. Particulars of my contingent assets not included in a previous Part of this Statement are as follows:—

DATED this   day of   19

....

Signature of Bankrupt.

What happens to income and property?

1. Income

A debtor may be expected to make contributions from income to the trustee during the bankruptcy, where there is a reasonable income surplus. If these voluntary payments are not made the trustee can apply for a court order forcing payment. Failure to make voluntary payment may also adversely affect any application for discharge. If a debtor's only source of income is a social security pension or benefit or a worker's compensation payment, contributions cannot be taken.

2. Exempt property

Under the Bankruptcy Act certain property is protected and cannot be sold by the trustee. This includes necessary clothing, necessary household property, tools of trade to the value of $2000 and certain insurance policies and annuities. It is important to note that any monies received by the bankrupt as damages or compensation, or any property substantially purchased with these funds, cannot be taken by the trustee.

3. Recoverable property

If the debtor, before becoming bankrupt, disposes of property or pays certain creditors in preference to other creditors such property and payments may be recoverable by the trustee.

4. Divisible property

Most property of any value, such as a house, car and video, will be sold. The proceeds are then distributed among the unsecured creditors, once the priority debts are paid.

If an asset such as a house is owned jointly the joint owner will usually be given the option of purchasing the bankrupt's equity in the property or joining the trustee in a sale. If there is little equity in the property it may be beneficial for a relative of the bankrupt to purchase this equity from the trustee. This may enable the bankrupt to still live in the property. Such an arrangement would require speedy action because as property values increase, so would the amount of equity in the property required to be purchased.

5. *Secured debts*

Secured creditors cannot realise any security as a result of the debtor becoming bankrupt. The bankrupt can continue to repay these debts, which may be secured by a home mortgage, a goods mortgage or a bill of sale over household items. But if the payments fall into arrears the creditors can repossess and sell the property.

If the property is sold and the proceeds are not enough to discharge the debt, then the creditor can be added to the list of unsecured creditors in the debtor's bankrupt estate. Also the trustee may decide to pay out small amounts owing on assets in order to sell them and distribute the proceeds in the estate. Co-borrowers and guarantors associated with the bankrupt's debts remain liable for these debts and the creditors can take legal action against them if the debtor fails to pay.

6. *Property acquired while bankrupt*

Assets, other than exempt property, which are acquired during the bankruptcy will be taken by the trustee. Such assets would include inheritances, lottery wins and superannuation. These possibilities must be fully considered before entering into bankruptcy.

7. *Property upon discharge*

Any property that vests in the trustee is not returned to the debtor once he or she is discharged from bankruptcy, unless there is a surplus or the trustee does not make a claim on this property within 20 years.

Consequences of bankruptcy

- A person who becomes bankrupt may be summoned to be examined about their financial affairs. Although this rarely occurs in a personal bankruptcy, it can be a difficult and humiliating experience for the debtor and needs to be considered.
- The debtor must disclose that he or she is an undischarged bankrupt if:
  - (a) application is made for credit of $500 or more;
  - (b) a cheque of $500 or more is written to pay for goods or services;
  - (c) a business is operated under an assumed name.

- A bankrupt must notify the Registrar and the trustee of any changes of address.

- A statement of earnings and details of expenditure must be given to the trustee each year.

- The bankrupt's passport must be relinquished, although in certain circumstances it may be regained.

- The bankruptcy will be noted on the files of the Credit Reference Association for seven years.

- The debtor must continue to pay court fines and family maintenance payments.

- Suppliers of household services, like telephone and electricity, may still disconnect these services for non-payment of arrears, regardless of the bankruptcy.

When does a bankruptcy end?

Automatic discharge from bankruptcy will occur after three years if no objections are made by the Registrar, the trustee or a creditor. These objections can extend the bankruptcy for a further two years and if the debtor wishes to obtain a discharge an application must be made to the court.

An application for discharge can also be made at any time after the bankrupt's public examination has been held or dispensed with, or one year after the date of bankruptcy.

Who can benefit from the Bankruptcy Act?

If a debtor has no possibility of repaying debts, is being harassed by creditors and has little to lose by way of income or assets, bankruptcy may be a viable option. Becoming bankrupt prevents creditors from contacting the debtor for payment of debts provable in the bankruptcy and once discharged, the person is generally no longer liable for these debts.

Under Part X of the Bankruptcy Act provision is also made for a debtor to come to a binding arrangement with any creditors without becoming bankrupt. There are three alternative arrangements:

1. A 'composition' where creditors agree to accept payments by instalments or less than the full amount in full settlement of the debt;
2. A 'deed of assignment' where the creditors agree to a transfer of the debtor's property, releasing the debtor from further payment;
3. A 'deed of arrangement' where the debtor's affairs are arranged in such a way as to pay the debts in whole or part.

Part X procedures are complex and expensive to administer. These arrangements are therefore mostly relevant to business debtors, rather than debtors who earn little income and who would constitute the majority of clients seen by financial counsellors.

A proposed legislative alternative to bankruptcy

Commonwealth legislation to provide an alternative to bankruptcy for consumer debtors is at present being drafted. This will be called the Regular Payment of Debts Scheme and would be applicable to insolvent, non-business debtors with debts of less than $30,000 (excluding home mortgages).

Under the Scheme, financial counsellors will assist debtors in formulating proposals to creditors which will include:

● a moratorium or temporary suspension of payments; or

● payment by instalments over a specified period, where the creditors are paid in full; or

● a composition paid by instalments, where the creditors receive less than full payment.

It is expected that the maximum period for these arrangements will be three years. Once a proposal for a plan is developed and approved by a financial counsellor, it would be forwarded to the Bankruptcy Administration. The administrator would then notify the creditors of the proposal. The plan could only be rejected by the creditors if a majority in number and value voted against it. Failure to reply within 21 days would be deemed as acceptance of the proposal.

The Regular Payment of Debts Scheme would provide a further option to financial counsellors in the alternatives considered in assisting a client experiencing financial difficulties.

Recommended reading:

Redfern Legal Centre's Lawyers Practice Manual (NSW) Sydney: Law Book Company Limited, 1983.

8

Workers' compensation

Each state and territory in Australia has workers' compensation legislation, which provides benefits for workers who suffer employment-related injuries. These injuries include partial and permanent incapacity, work-related diseases and death. Injuries can be the result of external and internal trauma to the body, for example cuts, abrasions, fractures and hernias, as well as diseases such as cancer, viral infections and mental illness.

Benefits may be received if the injury occurs at work; travelling between work, home, training school and/or medical treatment; and other circumstances specified in the various Acts. It is to be noted that a worker may not be entitled to compensation if there is a substantial deviation or interruption in the journey to or from work.

Compensation may be paid in the following ways:

- weekly payments;

- medical and hospital expenses;

- rehabilitation services;

- lump-sum payments:
    - for specific injuries such as loss of limbs, faculties (e.g. sight), sexual organs or facial disfigurement;
    - to dependants where injury results in death;
    - to redeem weekly payments.

An important aspect of workers' compensation is that payments are made irrespective of negligence on the part of the worker—although serious and wilful misconduct will disallow entitlement to compensation unless the injury results in death or serious and permanent disablement.

Although exactly who receives compensation and the amount and type of benefits provided by the legislation vary throughout Australia, a common feature is the hardship which can result from loss of health, work, income and self-esteem exacerbated by a protracted and complex system of law and court processes. Typical problems experienced by people caught in this system are highlighted in the following case study.

The problems of an injured worker

In 1984 Tony became one of the 111,606* new workers' compensation cases reported in New South Wales that year. He suffered a back injury when he slipped on a pool of oil that had leaked from one of the factory machines. Tony tried to continue working but the pain in his back increased. He had seen others injured on the factory machines and knew that if the problem worsened he must immediately report the injury to his employer, preferably in writing in the 'accident book'.

Tony went home and the next day found the pain in his back had increased. He made an appointment with his local doctor, who had seen such cases before and knew a certificate stating the cause of the injury and the period of incapacity would be required. The doctor told Tony to rest for two weeks and gave him a referral to a specialist.

The specialist prescribed medication for the pain and gave Tony a certificate stating that he was only fit for light duties. He approached his employer for light duties but there were none

---

*State Compensation Board, Workers' Compensation Statistics, NSW, year ended 30 June 1984.

available. Tony's future employment prospects were negligible, he had difficulty understanding English and his only work experience had been in unskilled, physically demanding jobs. He therefore completed a claim form for weekly compensation benefits, which he gave to his employer together with his medical certificates, and receipts for his doctor's bills and medication. He was correctly advised by one of his workmates to keep a copy of these papers. As required, the employer forwarded these documents to the insurer within seven days.

The first twelve months

For 26 weeks Tony received workers' compensation entitlements, which were equivalent to the weekly rate of wages provided by his award. He found it increasingly difficult to cope financially as the family had relied on his overtime at work to make ends meet.

Tony had been a very self-reliant man and proud to be the provider for his wife and three children aged two, five and ten years. As the months passed, the pain in his back worsened, he became depressed and there were marital and family problems.

After the first 26 weeks, Tony's workers' compensation entitlements dropped to a fixed amount prescribed by the Workers' Compensation Act, which included additional amounts for his wife and children. He then received notification from his employer that his contract of employment had been terminated and he would therefore not be entitled to annual leave payments. Tony had been relying on this money to pay some of his mounting bills.

Tony became increasingly frustrated, bitter and angry. He did not understand why he had to be subjected to the endless examinations of doctors who did not care for him. He did not know that when the insurance company requested examinations they should arrange and pay for a qualified interpreter to be present. Nor was he aware of the assistance provided by the Compensation Board's Ethnic Affairs Unit or the Rehabilitation Unit. But it had been made clear to him that unless he went to these medical examinations his compensation payments would probably stop until he did attend.

Tony had sold his car to help pay for the rent on his flat. The loss of the vehicle was another blow to Tony as this had represented his last vestige of self-reliance and freedom. He had to take taxis to his doctors' appointments and this meant his children having to forgo school excursions. Tony was not told that he was entitled to a refund for his travelling expenses as well as his medical and hospital costs.

Towards the end of the first year, the insurance company sent an assessor to question Tony about his injury and unwittingly Tony made statements without an interpreter or other reliable adult present. He then signed the statement and did not request a copy from the assessor.

The following week, Tony noticed a van parked across the street and found that films were being taken of his movements. Soon after, he was notified by the insurance company that they would no longer accept liability. As compensation payments had been paid for a year, the insurance company gave Tony the required six weeks' notice of intention to stop payments.

Tony immediately applied for a sickness benefit, not realising at the time that this benefit would have to be repaid from any compensation settlement he received. Nor did he realise that he was actually eligible for an unemployment benefit and that he should have been registered with the Commonwealth Employment Service with a view to obtaining employment. The unemployment benefit would generally not be repayable from a compensation settlement.

The lump-sum redemption

A friend of Tony's referred him to a solicitor, who had 'done a good job' on her house conveyance. Tony did not know about the free legal advisory service or the legal aid program provided by the State Compensation Board. And he did not belong to a trade union, where a service is usually provided to injured workers to help them with their compensation claims.

The solicitor filed an Application for Determination in the Compensation Court and advised Tony that it would be approximately 12 months before his case would be heard. He would 'just have to be patient'.

Finally he was contacted by his solicitor who advised that a lump-sum redemption had been offered by the insurance company. Although Tony was advised that a lump-sum redemption meant a 'once and for all' payment and he would no longer be entitled to weekly workers' compensation payments or any future medical expenses, he was desperate. His wife was expecting another baby and he had received an eviction order for non-payment of rent.

Tony went before the Compensation Court of New South Wales and agreed to accept the lump-sum redemption. The required approval was also given by the court.

With the compensation monies Tony paid his rent arrears and other outstanding bills, and then purchased a modest house for the family. Although his solicitor's bill seemed excessive he did not know that a taxation of costs by officers of the Supreme Court was possible. Nor was he aware that the Law Society could give him an indication of whether the bill seemed reasonable.

This was not the end of Tony's problems. He was still incapacitated for any work except light duties, all the compensation money had been spent, and he now found himself ineligible for sickness benefits as a result of the lump-sum redemption.

He was desperate and obtained a part-time job waiting on tables in his cousin's coffee shop. This work was painful for him but at least it was sufficient income to feed and clothe his family. Then the medical expenses for his medication and physiotherapy began to mount. He had expected to pay off his two bankcards, store account and personal loan now that he no longer had to pay rent, but he found this impossible.

He felt that he could no longer cope with the financial strain and then came the bill for his wife's confinement and an unexpected letter from the Department of Social Security requesting repayment of the sickness benefits he had received. He contacted the Department, which referred him for financial counselling.

Financial counselling

In the financial counselling interview, it was discerned that all the outstanding commitments were in fact owed and were all in Tony's name. There was no possibility of Tony being able to repay his debts from the income received from his part-time job at the coffee shop, which in any case he felt he could not physically keep doing for much longer. On further enquiry with the Department of Social Security it was found that he would probably be eligible for an unemployment benefit.

Tony decided that voluntary bankruptcy would be his most practical alternative in relation to his debts. Because his house had been purchased with the proceeds of his compensation settlement, it could not be taken by the trustee to pay his debts. This meant that the family could keep the house and the harassment of creditors would cease as future contact would have to be made through the trustee.

Becoming bankrupt also protected Tony's necessary household goods from being seized and sold to pay his debts, and contributions could not be sought from his unemployment benefits by the trustee. Further, the Department of Social Security could not withhold entitlement from his unemployment benefit in order to repay the sickness benefit received, and the Department became another unsecured creditor in the bankrupt estate.

The counsellor found that although income tax had been deducted from Tony's weekly compensation payments, he had not completed an income tax return, which would provide a substantial refund. Emergency assistance was obtained for the family in the form of food vouchers from the Food for Babies Fund, and application made for a family income supplement for which they would be eligible until a pension or benefit became available. As the eldest child had now started secondary school, an application was also made to the NSW Department of Education for a secondary bursary grant and textbook allowance.

As the history of Tony's accident and subsequent problems unfolded, it was found that there was a possibility of a claim for damages at common law. It seemed to have been reasonable to expect the employer to ensure the connection of a safety cap to the machine preventing the leakage of oil on which Tony had slipped.

He was referred to a legal adviser at the State Compensation Board, with a qualified interpreter, to consider the possibility of such a claim and to check that the lump-sum redemption did not preclude his rights at common law. Although any workers' compensation payments would be repayable to the insurance company out of any damages received, the advantage of a successful claim would be that Tony would be compensated not only for loss of income, medical and other expenses, but also for pain and suffering, loss of enjoyment of life and loss of expectation of life. Therefore the time and expense involved in such an action would be worthwhile.

The financial counsellor also made an appointment for Tony with a rehabilitation service, where he was given expert vocational counselling. He started a retraining program and learned how to manage his back pain. As a result his self-esteem began to improve and his marriage and family life also benefited.

Recommended reading:

Guidebook to Workers' Compensation in Australia (4th edn) Sydney: CCH Australia Limited, 1984.

Department of Social Security *Workers' Compensation Legislation in Australia 1984* Canberra: Australian Government Publishing Service, 1985.

9

Case studies

CASE STUDY NUMBER 1

Family details

Client: Mrs Leanne Jones
Age: 35 years
Children: John, 12 years; Elsa, 7 years

Mrs Jones has recently been divorced after 15 years of marriage. She is experiencing social, emotional, health and financial problems.

Social, emotional and health factors

The two children live with Mrs Jones in the family home which they have owned for seven years.

Mrs Jones works in a full-time position as a clerk with ACD Insurance Company in the city. She also has a part-time cleaning job with a firm of contract cleaners. This second job is in the office block in which she works during the day and is for three hours, three evenings per week.

Mr Jones has moved to another state and Mrs Jones finds it difficult to cope with the children without his support. Elsa's schoolwork has deteriorated and she is constantly in trouble at school. John is upset because he has to mind his sister while his mother works. This means that he cannot attend football practice or spend time with his friends. Both children miss their father and the telephone bill has increased because of their long-distance calls to him.

Mrs Jones is feeling socially isolated. She finds it difficult to go out by herself after having a constant companion for so many years. She also lacks time and money. Her social support network mainly consists of her neighbours in the street, who she feels she can call on for help in any emergency.

Recently Mrs Jones was diagnosed as having a hernia. Her doctor has advised her to stop her cleaning job as it is exacerbating the problem. The reason she started this job was in order to keep the family home in the property settlement, and this is her main financial priority.

Financial position

Mr Jones agreed to transfer the property to Mrs Jones for $20,000 and there was already a $20,000 mortgage on the property. This meant that Mrs Jones had to borrow $40,000 to pay out Mr Jones and the existing mortgage. The most she could obtain at a reasonable rate of interest was $30,000 from a building society. The remaining $10,000 was borrowed from a finance company and secured by a second mortgage over the house. She also took out a cash advance of $1000 on Bankcard to help pay for the legal costs and stamp duty as she had insufficient savings after the cost of the divorce.

Mrs Jones bought a car in order to get to work as well as to help with shopping and to allow herself some social freedom. The suburb in which she lives is serviced by a local bus which runs hourly to the train station and shopping centre. She borrowed a personal loan of $3000 from a finance company, secured by a mortgage over the car.

At present Mrs Jones is overcommitted by $540 per month. The first mortgage is one month in arrears. The second mortgage is two months in arrears and legal action has been threatened by the finance company. The council and water rates are also due.

INCOME/EXPENDITURE SHEET
Client: Mrs Leanne Jones

Income

		Net per month
ADC Insurance Co.	$282 gross p.w.	$1 045
Help Cleaners	$93 gross p.w.	278
Family Allowance		55
	TOTAL	$1 378

Cash Expenses

	Monthly
Food	$390
Pocket money	43
Fares	87
Petrol	65
School	87
Entertainment	20
TOTAL	$692

Regular Bills

1st mortgage	$350
2nd mortgage	349
Council rates	20
Water rates	22
Electricity	55
Telephone	32
House insurance	13
Contents insurance	10
Car 3rd party insurance	7
Car registration	26
Bankcard	50
Personal loan	120
TOTAL	$1 054

Additional Expenses

Clothing	$100
Medical	5
Dental	10
House maintenance	25
Car maintenance	20
Gifts	12
TOTAL	$172

Total Expenditure	$1 918
Total Income	$1 378
Overcommitment	$540

Outstanding Debts

Debt	Creditor		Arrears	Balance	Term
1st mortgage (house)	AD	Building Society	$350	$30 000	25 yrs
2nd mortgage (house)	TS	Finance Company	698	10 000	4 yrs
Secured P/L (car)	GH	Finance Company	120	3 000	4 yrs
Bankcard	XY	Bank		1 000	
Council rates	JK	Council	240	240	
Water rates	RH	Water Board	264	264	

Assets

	Market Value
House	$75 000
Car	$4 500

Outcome of financial counselling

Through counselling Mrs Jones gained a greater understanding of her values, standards, goals and the pressures she was encountering. As a result she was able to see her situation more clearly and thereby reassess her priorities and substantially improve all aspects of her situation. She found that in order to keep her home, she had been unable to spend essential time with her children, her health had suffered and her financial position had become unmanageable.

Mrs Jones decided that her first priority must be the emotional and physical health of the children and herself, which included the maintenance of essential living expenditure. If at all possible she then wanted to keep the house, which provided necessary security in a neighbourhood with important social support networks. Although the car provided important freedom of movement, Mrs Jones could see that transport alternatives were possible and the accomplishment of her other goals was more important. Once these priorities were established, alternatives could be considered and decisions made by Mrs Jones.

1. Emotional and health factors

In order to improve her health and be able to spend more time with her children, Mrs Jones decided to stop her part-time cleaning job. It was suggested to Mrs Jones that a workers' compensation claim could be possible if the hernia was a work-related illness. She subsequently found that she was entitled to compensation and therefore continued to receive $93 gross per week.

Having more time with the children meant that Mrs Jones could help Elsa with her schoolwork and help John with his problems. An after-school care program was found for Elsa and this allowed John to spend time with his friends and the football coach who provided a male role model. The school counsellor was also made aware of Elsa's difficulties, which meant a more caring approach was taken towards her at school.

As Mrs Jones was having difficulty coping with her children

and coming to terms with her divorce, a referral was made for separation and family counselling. She was also put in touch with a local self-help group of lone parents, who could offer social and emotional support.

2. *Financial alternatives*

Mrs Jones decided to sell the car and obtained $4500 from the sale. With this money she paid out the secured finance company loan of $3000, discharged the bankcard debt of $1000 and cleared the arrears with the Council and Water Board. This substantially reduced expenditure in the areas of car maintenance, insurance, registration and petrol, as well as relieving the pressures of being behind in repayments. She also handed back the bankcard to ensure that the temptation of purchasing on credit would be removed.

The alternatives presented to Mrs Jones in relation to the house were:

(a) to sell and place the balance remaining in a secure income-producing investment or use the balance as a deposit on a unit; or

(b) obtain mortgage relief to clear arrears on the home loans and help maintain repayments while applying to the Co-operative Housing Societies' Special Eligibility Committee for a loan of $45,000 to discharge the existing first and second mortgages and help with legal costs and stamp duty.

As there were no affordable houses or units in the area where Mrs Jones lived, either for purchase or rental accommodation, selling the house would have meant moving to another area. The children would then need to change schools and the current neighbourhood support network would be lost. Mrs Jones therefore decided to try for the second alternative. She realised that if approved, the Co-operative loan would take at least a year to become available and therefore interim help would be needed from the first and second mortgagees. Also mortgage relief would have to be repaid.

The next consideration was possible decreases in expenditure in other areas. The release from the part-time job meant that Mrs Jones no longer relied so heavily on fast foods. She now had more time to shop, cook and prepare the children's lunches. This meant a substantial saving in food expenditure.

When developing her money plan, Mrs Jones discussed the financial situation with the children and everyone's needs were considered. As a result John decided to obtain a part-time job on a paper run. This meant he no longer required pocket-money and could pay for his own outings and haircuts.

There was little room for increases in income as extra work was not possible with Mrs Jones' health problem and the need to be with her children, although she did think that when her situation improved she might do a part-time course to improve her prospects for a better paying job.

Because of the property settlement agreed upon by Mr and Mrs Jones, he was not required to pay family maintenance. Nevertheless, through counselling, Mrs Jones was able to become more objective about her situation and the needs of the family, and was able to obtain Mr Jones' agreement to the children telephoning him by reverse charge twice a week and to his paying $50 per month towards their clothing expenses. On considering shopping alternatives, Mrs Jones also felt that she could reduce her expenditure on clothing.

These alternatives led to the following money plan being developed:

MONEY PLAN

Net Income	Net per week
ADC Insurance Co.	$241
Workers' compensation	64
Family allowance	13
Total income	$318

Cash Expenses	
Food	$80
Pocket money	5
Fares	20
School	10
Personal	5
Entertainment	10
1. Total cash from income	$130

Regular Bills	
Mortgages	$100
Council rates	5
Water rates	5
Electricity	13
Telephone	5
House insurance	3
Contents insurance	2
2. Total in bill-paying account	$133

Additional Expenses	
Clothing	$10
Medical	1
Dental	2
House maintenance	6
Gifts	3
3. Total in expenses account	$22

Total Income	$318
Total Expenses	$285
Surplus	$33

CASE STUDY NUMBER 2

Family details

Names:		*Ages:*	
	Danny Cross		27 years
	Rhonda Cross		26 years
	Harry Cross		6 years
	Louise Cross		3 years

Social, emotional and health factors

The Cross family live in a new two-bedroom brick veneer house. They purchased this property six months ago after their best friends bought a house at a similar new housing estate in an isolated suburb of Sydney.

Mr Cross works shiftwork from 10 pm to 6 am at a factory which is five kilometres from home. Three weeks ago Mrs Cross lost her part-time job as a waitress at a local fast food outlet, where she worked for 20 hours per week. She has no other work experience or training, and employment is very scarce in the area even if she did seek other work.

No one in the family is well. They all keep catching colds. Harry has very high dental bills. Louise suffers severe asthma attacks. Mr Cross is smoking heavily due to strain and Mrs Cross is taking Serapax for her nerves.

Mrs Cross dislikes grocery shopping, which she finds difficult to do with the children. She never seems to have enough money for the food, especially now that she can no longer bring home pizzas and hamburgers four nights a week from the take-away restaurant where she worked. She buys everything at the local shop and cooks using convenient packet and tinned food.

Mr Cross goes to the local club every Saturday evening. Mrs Cross resents being left at home to mind the children and is feeling very isolated and lonely. She is also angry that he spends $25 on drinks when the bills at home remain unpaid. Mr and Mrs Cross are fighting every day and Mr Cross has threatened to leave several times.

Financial position

The expense of purchasing the house was much greater than Mr
and Mrs Cross had expected. The finance was arranged by the
real estate agent through two finance companies and all of their
savings were used to pay the deposit, legal costs and stamp duty.
Because the house was new they wanted to fill it with new furniture and the most modern electrical appliances. For these expenses they used a department store account and bankcard.

Mr Cross insists that the car payment is an absolute priority
although he has lost his licence for six months because of driving
under the influence of alcohol and speeding. He has been fined
$500. Because there is no public transport to and from his work
at the hours he requires, he relies on his car. Rhonda has never
learnt to drive as this frightens her.

The electricity account, dental bill, reminders for three loan
repayments, Bankcard and an ambulance bill of $86 have all
arrived at once. They are two months behind with their second
mortgage and the mortgagee has threatened legal action.

Outcome of financial counselling

In counselling much time was spent in considering the needs of
each member of the family. Mr and Mrs Cross had conflicting
priorities and goals. For example, Mr Cross saw the car as his
first priority even though he had lost his licence and could not
drive the car for six months, and for Mrs Cross the first priority
was the house.

Once they attained a clearer understanding of each other's
needs and wants, and an appreciation of the values and standards
affecting their decisions, they were able to start considering
viable alternatives.

In reassessing their priorities, they decided that their marriage
and children must come first and that this would mean a drastic
change in their financial priorities. Mr and Mrs Cross agreed that
the house provided a necessary element of security and stability

INCOME/EXPENDITURE SHEET
Clients: Mr and Mrs Cross

Income	Net per month
Mr Cross $400 gross per week	$1 391
Family Allowance	55
TOTAL	**$1 446**

Cash Expenses	Monthly
Food	$650
Fares	26
Petrol	87
School	20
Cigarettes	121
Alcohol	108
TOTAL	**$1 012**

Regular Bills	
1st Mortgage	$450
2nd Mortgage	289
Council rates	20
Water rates	22
Electricity	55
Telephone	32
Health fund	66
House insurance	8
Contents insurance	8
Car 3rd party insurance	6
Car registration	30
Bankcard	56
Department store account	47
Personal loan	382
TOTAL	**$1 471**

Additional Expenses	
Clothing	$100
Medical	10
Dental	20
House maintenance	35
Car maintenance	33
Gifts	20
TOTAL	**$218**

Total Expenditure	$2 701
Total Income	$1 446
Overcommitment	$1 255

Outstanding Debts

Debt	Creditor	Arrears	Balance	Term
1st Mortgage	HY Finance Company	$450	$26 000	15 yrs
2nd Mortgage	GL Finance Company	578	14 000	10 yrs
Secured P/L (car)	LI Finance Company		10 000	3 yrs
Bankcard	XZ Bank	56	600	
Charge account	WT Department Store	47	500	
Electricity	SS County Council	164	164	
Fine	Police Department	500	500	
Dental bill	Dr Ray	300	300	
Ambulance bill	Z District Ambulance	86	86	

Assets	Market Value
House	$50 000
Car	$10 000

for the family and to sell would mean moving to another suburb and Harry having to change schools. But when an income/expenditure sheet was completed they realised that it might not be financially possible to keep the house.

1. Financial alternatives

Once it was ascertained that all the debts were in fact owing and the calculations of the repayments, balances and pay-out figures were checked and rechecked, action could be taken to bring the income/outgo position into balance. Mr Cross contacted all of their creditors and requested that they allow one month for him to reorganise his financial affairs. He obtained agreements to this and confirmed his arrangements in writing with the help of the counsellor. Through this process Mr Cross attained a sense of control over his situation.

The car: Mr and Mrs Cross decided to sell the car. With the proceeds of the sale they were able to pay out the secured finance company loan of $10,000. This meant a saving of $382 per month plus the additional expenses of registration, insurance, petrol and car maintenance. Mr Cross was able to obtain a lift to and from work with a neighbour who had recently moved to the same housing estate. This only cost $10 per week towards petrol.

The house: The counsellor found that Mr and Mrs Cross were eligible for a grant under the First Home Ownership Scheme. This meant they could obtain a lump sum of $3000 plus a monthly loan repayment subsidy. With this assistance it was decided that it would be feasible to apply for a loan from a bank or building society to discharge the first and second mortgages with the finance companies. If this was not possible, they realised that the house would have to be sold immediately in order to retain the small amount of equity still left in the property.

Mr and Mrs Cross applied for and were granted the First Home Ownership assistance, and after approaching several banks and building societies they were able to obtain a loan at a reasonable interest rate to discharge the existing mortgages. The

$3000 lump sum helped them to pay for the stamp duty and legal costs associated with obtaining a new mortgage.

Outstanding commitments: The lump sum also enabled them to pay their electricity account and speeding fine as well as pay out their department store and bankcard debts. Mr and Mrs Cross did not realise that they were paying into the highest cover in their private medical fund, as this was deducted weekly from Mr Cross' pay packet. On further investigation it was found that most of the dental and ambulance bills could be claimed from the health fund.

2. Social, emotional and health factors

Once the pressing financial problems were alleviated, Mr and Mrs Cross could start dealing with other areas of their lives. Their self-esteem had greatly improved through their successful negotiations with their creditors and they started feeling more in control of their situation. Developing mutual priorities and goals had greatly increased their communication and they wanted to do more to improve their relationship. An appropriate referral for ongoing marital counselling was made.

Mr Cross could see how the family and financial pressures were affecting his health through excess smoking. He decided to cut down to three packets a week and to consider one of the quit-smoking programs suggested by the financial counsellor. He also obtained a part-time job at the club on Friday afternoons. This gave him a necessary social outlet and meant that instead of spending $25 per week on alcohol, he was earning an extra $40 net per week.

Mr and Mrs Cross decided they needed to spend some time alone together and that they would save $50 per month for a special night out at their favourite restaurant.

The counsellor considered cooking and shopping alternatives with Mr and Mrs Cross. A weekly food budget was arranged with a shopping list and some simple, nutritious recipes. An occasional care centre was found near a reasonably priced supermarket, so that the children could be cared for while Mrs Cross did the shopping. Mrs Cross also enrolled in courses on nutrition, budget meal preparation and shopping skills available at the local Community Health Centre. She later joined a stress management and relaxation course which helped her become increasingly less reliant on the Serapax as well as providing a needed social outlet.

The development of these skills meant that Mrs Cross started to enjoy the weekly shopping and found that she could be quite creative in preparing meals; the shopping bill was also reduced to $90 per week. The improved nutrition soon meant that the family's health began to improve. The reduction in sugar intake would probably also improve Harry's teeth in the long run, and it was found that he was eligible for free treatment at the dental clinic through the school.

Mr and Mrs Cross were put in touch with the Asthma Foundation of New South Wales, for advice and support with Louise's health problem. The counsellor also referred them to a poly-clinic, which provided services such as counselling and free swimming lessons to asthma sufferers.

The Crosses decided that their goals would be to save for a family holiday and a deposit for a reasonably priced car. To help achieve these goals the following money plan was developed:

MONEY PLAN

	Net per week
Net Income	
Mr Cross	$321
FE Club	40
Family Allowance	13
Total income	$374
Cash Expenses	
Food	$90
Fares	16
School	5
Cigarettes	6
Personal	10
Entertainment	12
1. Total cash from income	$139
Regular Bills	
House mortgage	$104
Council rates	5
Water rates	5
Electricity	13
Telephone	7
Health fund	15
House insurance	2
Contents insurance	2
2. Total in bill-paying account	$153
Additional Expenses	
Clothing	$23
Medical	2
Dental	5
House maintenance	8
Gifts	5
3. Total in expenses account	$43
Total Income	$374
Total Expenses	$335
Surplus	$39
+ First Home Owners subsidy	$12
Total Savings	$51

CASE STUDY NUMBER 3

Family details

> *Client:* Miss Helen Holmes
> *Age:* 19 years

Social, emotional and health factors

For a year Miss Holmes shared a unit with her boyfriend, Jim. He left her three months ago when she found that she was three months pregnant. She has not heard from Jim since that time and does not know where he can be located. She has remained in the unit by herself in the hope that Jim would return. As the rental is $120 per week, her savings have now been depleted and she needs to find alternative accommodation.

Miss Holmes is the eldest of five children. Her parents are invalid pensioners who live in a housing commission flat in an outer suburb of Sydney. Miss Holmes left home when she was 16 years old and does not consider that her family is able to offer any emotional or financial support. She has a small group of friends her own age, but as she is no longer able to go to pubs and nightclubs regularly with them, they are beginning to lose contact and she is becoming increasingly isolated.

Financial position

Miss Holmes is working in a local supermarket but will have to terminate her employment in four weeks and apply for a Special Benefit from the Department of Social Security. She has no sick pay or holiday pay owing to her when she leaves work, nor is she eligible for maternity leave.

When she moved into the unit with Jim, they took out joint accounts to buy furniture and appliances. They now have an account with a department store for $1500 and a bankcard debt of $2000. Both accounts are three months in arrears and the creditors have threatened legal action. As Jim cannot be located, Miss Holmes has been left with the responsibility of paying these bills.

The following income/expenditure sheet is based on the income Miss Holmes will be receiving when she leaves work and

INCOME/EXPENDITURE SHEET
Client: Miss Helen Holmes

Income		*Net per month*	
Special benefit $102 gross per week		$442	
Cash Expenses		*Monthly*	
Food		$217	
Fares		43	
Entertainment		20	
Personal		22	
	TOTAL	$302	
Regular Bills			
Rent		$520	
Electricity		30	
Telephone		20	
Contents insurance		10	
Bankcard		100	
Department store account		150	
	TOTAL	$830	
Additional Expenses			
Clothing		20	
Medical/pharmaceutical		20	
Dental		10	
	TOTAL	$50	
Total Expenditure		$1182	
Total Income		$442	
Overcommitment		$740	

Outstanding Debts

Debt	*Creditor*	*Arrears*	*Balance*
Bankcard	XY Bank	$300	$2000
Charge account	WT Department Store	$450	$1500

the minimum monthly repayments currently due on the bank-card and department store accounts. This shows that Miss Holmes is overcommitted by $740 per month.

Outcome of financial counselling

Miss Holmes decided that her main priority was to care for her child on a full-time basis. She did not expect to see Jim again and realised that a drastic change in lifestyle would be needed to accomplish her goal.

1. Social, emotional and health factors

Miss Holmes was referred to the hospital social worker and a local pregnancy support group for counselling and assistance.

As she needed a supportive environment and was eager to learn new living skills to cope with child rearing, the financial counsellor suggested that an accommodation alternative might be a new group living home for single mothers. Miss Holmes thought that this would be an excellent option as she would have the companionship of four other single mothers living in the home. Further, it was affordable because expenses would be shared and she would be able to participate in the living skills program provided at the home by various experts from the community. The program would include developing skills in money management, shopping, cooking, nutrition and crafts. Another important factor was that the house was located in her local area and she could continue to see the same doctor and counsellor, as well as maintain contact with her friends.

2. Financial alternatives

Miss Holmes was accepted into the group home. This meant that when she left work, she would be able to survive on the special benefit until she became eligible for the supporting parent's benefit.

Once it was established that Miss Holmes was responsible for the department store and bankcard debts, an arrangement was negotiated with these creditors. They agreed to freeze the interest on the accounts and allow a one-month moratorium on repayments while Miss Holmes sorted out her financial position. The Credit Reference Association was also contacted to ensure that Jim's credit file was separated from Helen's.

The alternatives available to Miss Holmes in relation to these debts included:

- To sell the furniture and appliances to repay the debts.

- To negotiate with the creditors to write off the debts or freeze the interest and accept a nominal repayment over an extended period.

- If the creditors would not assist, the matter could be referred to the Commissioner for Consumer Affairs as the contracts were regulated by the Credit Act (NSW).

- Miss Holmes could enter voluntary bankruptcy. As her only source of income would be a social security benefit she would not be required to make contributions from her income and the debts would be automatically discharged in three years.

Miss Holmes decided that she wanted to repay her debts and avoid entering bankruptcy. As she would not need the furniture and appliances, which were already provided in the group home, she decided to sell as much as possible. These were purchased by her friends and neighbours in her block of units. With the proceeds of sale, she was able to repay the majority of the debts and the creditors agreed to write off the balances outstanding.

The owner of the unit in which Miss Holmes lived agreed to accept the four weeks rental bond as a final rental payment and Miss Holmes moved into the group home at the end of this four-week period.

In the group home the payment for rent, electricity, insurance and maintenance amounted to $50 per week. The alternatives decided upon in financial counselling led to the following money plan being developed. It is to be noted that once Miss Holmes is eligible for the supporting parent's benefit, rental allowance and family allowance, she will have an income surplus enabling her to save for her goals.

MONEY PLAN	
Net Income	*Net per week*
Special benefit	$102
Cash Expenses	
Food	$20
Fares	5
Personal	5
Entertainment	10
1. Total cash from income	$40
Regular Bills	
Rent	$50
Telephone	5
2. Total in bill-paying account	$55
Additional Expenses	
Clothing	$5
Medical/dental	2
3. Total in expenses account	$7
Total Income	$102
Total Expenses	$102

This case study highlights the untenable financial position of many single parents, most of whom would not have access to a group home situation. Their alternatives are therefore often to pay 80 per cent of their income for rent while waiting, sometimes many years, for housing commission accommodation.